10 Women Adventurers Who Reached the Top

Life-changing Biographies for Teens and Young Adults

Ariana Smith

Copyright © 2023 Ariana Smith. All rights reserved.

The contents of this book may not be reproduced, duplicated, or transmitted without direct written permission from the author.

Under no circumstances will any legal responsibility or blame be held against the publisher for any reparation, damages, or monetary loss due to the information herein, either directly or indirectly.

Legal Notice:

This book is copyright protected. This is only for personal use. You can't amend, distribute, sell, use, quote, or paraphrase any part of the content within this book without the consent of the author.

Disclaimer Notice:

Please note the information contained within this document is for educational and entertainment purposes only. Every attempt has been made to provide accurate, up to date, and reliable complete information. No warranties of any kind are expressed or implied. Readers acknowledge that the author is not engaging in the rendering of legal, financial, medical, or professional advice. The content of this book has been derived from various sources.

By reading this document, the reader agrees that under no circumstances is the author responsible for any losses, direct or indirect, which are incurred as a result of the use of information contained within this document, including, but not limited to, errors, omissions, or inaccuracies.

ISBN 978-9916-9880-4-6 (eBook)
ISBN 978-9916-9880-3-9 (paperback)
ISBN 978-9916-9880-2-2 (hardcover)

www.ariana-smith.com

Contents

Introduction	1
What Does Being an Adventurer Entail?	4
1. Isabella Lucy Bird	13
2. Maria Spelterini	25
3. Hélène de Pourtalès	33
4. Annie Londonderry	43
5. Tiny Broadwick	55
6. Eva Dickson	67
7. Gertrude Ederle	79
8. Krystyna Chojnowska	93
9. Junko Tabei	105
10. Donna Tobias	115
Setting Achievable Goals	124
Conclusion	131

Introduction

The definition of 'adventure' is 'an unusual and exciting or daring experience.'

For thrill-seekers, explorers, and adrenaline-junkies, adventure is perhaps their core principle in life. Adventurers choose to live on the edge and take risks, although all the while knowing that there's certainly an element of danger involved.

They are not satisfied with only going to school, getting a job, getting married, having kids, retiring, and then passing-on according to nature's timing. Instead, they want to feel everything that being human means; they want to push their bodies, minds, and emotions to the limits, as a way to truly determine what they're capable of; as a way to truly harness and manifest the strength of the human body, of human willpower, and their ability to outsmart fear.

The risks they take are usually well calculated, bar unexpected scenarios. Never underestimate the intelligence of an adventurer. This intelligence is, indeed, what separates the aspect of adventure from sheer stupidity.

It begins with an idea that is fast accompanied by a feeling of exhilaration, as the adventurer sees themselves not only at the finish-line with a personal lifetime achievement award, but also stronger than they've *ever* been, which boosts serotonin in the brain, enhancing self-esteem and a sense of fulfilment.

The adventurer knows, both during and once they've completed their task, that they're demonstrating something others might not have the skill, courage, will and initiative to achieve—although they probably could if they wanted to. And that's the key for adventurers; they really *want* to achieve what they set out to do.

True adventurers are dreamers. They don't choose to put themselves through trauma and risk death for logic, although logic plays a crucial role in the steps they'll take.

People with the spirit of fire, those who defy 'tip-toe' or 'play it safe' rules, often become adventurers. Perhaps it's the physical 'pushing themselves to the limits' ideal driving them. Often, it's being 'the first to accomplish a task' that becomes the driving factor. At other times, it is sheer curiosity as to whether or not they *can* achieve what they've set out to, knowing if they succeed, they will forever be stronger than they thought they were.

Seldom do people become adventurers to prove something to others. Adventurers are not egotistical, boastful beings. In fact, many of them are quite humble about their achievements in public. They do it for themselves, mostly—as a way to live life to the fullest and, hopefully, in the end, they'll be able to put themselves to rest knowing they did just about everything they wanted to, without hurting others along the way.

An adventurer is not selfish, nor is an adventurer crazy. An adventurer is born with a deep and passionate wanderlust for new experiences, with a desire to want to feel life differently. And if through their story they can make an impression on, and urge, others to take similar calculated risks in order to feel the thrill that is the birthright of all humans, they are more often than not very happy with this.

This is why many adventurers become 'Legends.' They leave behind legacies of bravery, daring, and audacity which help others to realize their own limitations and become strong enough within themselves to set their own goals through adventurous tasks aimed at helping them self-manifest their core power.

In this book we take a look at some of the very first women to achieve the unthinkable, in a time when women were mostly seen as mothers or housewives, having to complete mandatory tasks and watch time go by without ever feeling what it really means to be alive.

What Does Being an Adventurer Entail?

Seldom do people suddenly wake-up one morning and decide they want to climb Mount Everest. In most cases, they have either displayed the adventurer spirit throughout their lives, or they have been given some kind of ultimatum on their lifespan.

This is not to say that only certain people can become adventurers. Of course, anyone can attempt to do things they've not done before, no matter how extreme. But without the passion and drive for what they're doing they'll likely only get halfway before giving up.

It's important to note that extreme acts of daring are not to be carried out as a way to prove to someone that you're more than they think you are. People will think what they want of you, whether you're a stay-at-home-mom or free-diver; if someone does not like you, they're going to criticize everything you do, even if you save the world!

Committing to the adventure is not something any adventurer can do without facing doubt. Of course, doubt inevitably rears its head, mostly because, well, unless they're a suicidal Kamikaze pilot, they certainly intend to live through the experience! But every adventure bears risk, and even the threat to life.

Being an adventurer does not mean the person is fearless. Rather it means they have enough intelligence to be able to both foresee and prepare for unexpected circumstances; a little like flying with two parachutes in case the first does not open.

And so, the driving principle behind achieving something out of the ordinary should be one's personal sense of achievement and fulfilment. Adventurers do what they do for self-gratification (although this can't be seen as selfish); seldom is it for fame or fortune. Fame and fortune become by-products of their bravery.

So, what does it take to be a true adventurer with the Spirt of Fire for that which, to others, seems far too daunting to even consider?

Here are some of the most important aspects or characteristics required to be a true adventurer.

1. Curiosity

Adventures more often than not are initiated through curiosity. 'How would it feel to do such-and-such'? 'Am I capable of embarking on such a journey or facing such a challenge'? Or even, 'What does the view look like from the top of that mountain'? In most cases, the final adventure chosen by the adventurer begins with curiosity about it.

2. A Personal Goal

Adventurers are also driven achievers, in the sense that succeeding in their specific adventure would fulfil a certain personal goal. They seldom do what they do to 'boast' or 'prove others wrong.' Most of the time, they do what they do to prove something to themselves, or to feel accomplished at having overcome the challenges presented by their chosen adventure task.

3. Willpower

Willpower is one of the most important qualities an adventurer needs in meeting their goal, especially if the task they have chosen is life-threatening. Indeed, it is triumphing over these threats which brings about the feeling adventurers seek. Willpower is what keeps them walking against the blizzard or forcing their muscles to act despite the burn.

In fact, it can be very difficult to convince an adventurer to turn back or abort their mission, due to their power of will; the narrative they have programed themselves with as a means to never back down. This is why it is so important for the adventurer to have a good support team, because the individual can become obsessed with achievement and, thus, place themselves in grave danger. Their support team will be perfectly aware of the individual's capabilities and will be firm enough with them when the time comes to tell them to stop—if such times ever arise.

4. A Specific Set of Skills

It would be unwise to attempt to swim the English Channel if you are not a trained swimmer. Likewise, someone who chooses to walk the length of the Australian Outback on foot would need to know how to identify animal tracks and venomous creatures, for example, as well as how to save water. And so, if it becomes an individual's goal to achieve something specific, they will need to either already be trained in their task or spend a certain amount of time learning the skills needed to successfully accomplish it.

5. Passion

As the individual plans their adventure, they will wake up each day fulfilled by their goal. If the individual at any point states, "Oh, I don't need to do this today, I can continue tomorrow," they do not have the amount of passion needed to accomplish their task. Of course, there may be days when unexpected scenarios arise, but in cases like these, the individual would feel a little disgruntled at not being able to take the steps they need to, in order to meet their goal. This is passion; passion is being so driven by a goal upon waking each day that it seems to be all you live for. If your goal is secondary, it's unlikely you'll find yourself putting your all towards it.

6. Determination and Tenacity

One of the requirements towards reaching a goal is determination. Beyond this determination, the individual will need to display tenacity, which means they won't only need to continue to convince themselves mentally that such-and-such has to be achieved, they actually physically have to get up and do it.

This is tenacity—not giving-up. Determination can be considered the mental partner to physical tenacity. At the same time, however, it will be important to set achievable goals from the start, so that you experience the sense of achievement, which will drive you to want to take the next step toward your goal. If you set your initial goals too high, there may be risk of failure which will leave you feeling defeated. It will also be important to pace yourself, meaning you will need to create a plan of action and stick to it; one that won't see you burn out or face doubt.

7. Focus and Concentration

As stated previously, your adventure task goal should be the primary focus of your life, not secondary. If you don't have the time or resources to achieve it at the start, you can continue to plan, but you will need to wait for the right time for it to be your sole-focus. In most cases, the dream arrives in the mind of the individual. Because of it, they begin to explore different ways of approaching the proposed goal.

This is preparation time, and preparations can begin even while the task is still secondary to the individual. However, when the time comes closer to the initiation of the task, those months and weeks will need all the individual's attention. They may need to put certain activities, people, or responsibilities aside, in order to keep their focus. Once again, this is why having a support team is vital. The people you live with or who are closely connected to will, preferably, support you by giving you the time and space you need to concentrate on your goal.

8. A Healthy Lifestyle

Focusing on a healthy lifestyle will ensure you have balance in your life, because balance is very important for a healthy life. If you will be using your body to the extreme before and during your adventure, it will need to be fit and functioning. You cannot function at your best, for example, if you have digestion issues.

Likewise, if you cannot pull your own body weight from the ground and hold it suspended for a certain amount of time, you will not be able to climb a cliff face. Health is, therefore, very important to an adventurer, and this goes for mental health as well.

9. Correct Use of Time

Being an adventurer does not mean you can come and go as you please. A true adventurer will have set themselves a list of goals and effectively concluded which steps they need to take in order to reach them. Working with time is an important skill too; and an example of this would be if you need to train to be able to withstand cold conditions. For, say, a walk across the Arctic shelf on snowshoes, a first step would be to spend time training in cold conditions.

Likewise, the adventurer will use their time wisely; if they want to run five miles on a particular day but it begins to rain, they won't waste time in sitting around waiting for the rain to stop. Instead, they'll already have an alternative activity ready to complete while it is raining. This is commonly known as always having a Plan B. Having a Plan A and a Plan B allows for environmental changes without time being wasted.

Routine is important to an adventurer too, as it is through routine that our biological clocks are set; when we wake up, when we eat, what time of day we choose to exercise, and so forth. Choosing to become an adventurer does not mean you just wake up free to do what you want to. Adventures are always following some kind of plan, to ensure no time is wasted in the pursuit of their goal.

10. Authenticity and Legitimacy

There is no use in telling others that you intend to climb Mount Everest if your only intention is to make them think you have an adventurous heart. An adventurer is not a manipulator, nor do they aim to impress others. They aim to impress themselves and be taken seriously. To get the assistance they need to fulfil their goals, they will need to show their authenticity and be able to set boundaries for themselves.

If someone tells an adventurer that they will support their journey only 'if they do such and such,' but the adventurer does not agree, then they must be strong enough to say, "As much as I need the assistance, I'm not prepared to do that." Also, an adventurer will not boast about past achievements without actually having done those things. This is what separates liars from truth-tellers. So, having a clean record in maintaining authenticity and legitimacy helps the adventurer to gain more support in achieving their goal from those who want to help them. This issue is related to earning grants or sponsorships for different adventures (via crowdfunding, for instance). A true adventurer needs to remain honest and humble—although keeping smart and humorous is never a bad idea if it is authentic, and through this, they will win respect and support.

Isabella Lucy Bird

1831 - 1904

"I have just dropped into the very place I have been seeking, but in everything it exceeds all my dreams."
~ Isabella Lucy Bird

Who was Isabella?

Isabella Lucy Bird was born on October 15th, 1831, at Boroughbridge Hall, Yorkshire, England. Her father, Reverend Edward Bird, fulfilled his curacy, taking holy orders in 1821. Isabella moved home a few times during her childhood, from Maidenhead in Berkshire to Tattenhall in Cheshire, where her sister, Henrietta, was born.

Lucy was very outspoken and knowledgeable as a young girl, a trait she carried with her throughout her life. At just six-years-old, she asked the local MP for South Cheshire, *"Did you tell my father my sister was so pretty because you wanted his vote?"*[1]

Edward was not too popular among the authorities because he advocated to have Sundays a 'rest day' not a labor day. After having insults, stones, and mud thrown at him, the family moved again, for a short while to the Southern coastal resort of Eastbourne, and then on to Wyton in Huntingdonshire, currently known as Cambridgeshire.

Although Isabella was clever, she was considered a frail child, suffering with spinal complaints, nervous headaches, and also insomnia. Back then, there was no certain medication available for these ailments, but doctors recommended that she be outdoors in the fresh air as often as possible. And so, she rode horses from an early age, and also learned to row boats.

She was raised by her parents, with her father helping her to focus on botany, and her mother teaching her an array of eclectic subjects. Isabella loved to read but was easily distracted. Perhaps today she might have been diagnosed with Attention Deficit Disorder (ADHD). No matter how bright and precocious her intelligence, it seemed impossible for anyone to train her within such a strictly evangelical environment.

At age sixteen she wrote her first article, a pamphlet, focusing on 'free trade versus protectionism.' After this, she wrote numerous articles on subjects of importance to her and the world around her.

By 1850, doctors had discovered a fibrous tumor around her spine which they were able to remove, although Isabella still suffered with lassitude—a lack of energy—and insomnia. Due to this, her family spent six summers in Scotland, in an attempt to improve these complications.

Although that helped a little, it was further recommended that she take to the seas and spend some time on a cruise in the open waters. With her second cousins about to travel by ship to the US at the time, she joined them. Her father gave her money and said he would support her for as long as it took for her health to improve. This journey was where it all began for Isabella's writing career, as she would write letters to her family back home which would ultimately become the basis of her first book, *An Englishwoman in America*, in 1856.

After having returned to Britain for a while, she ventured out again in 1872, this time to Australia, and then to Hawaii, which were known as the 'Sandwich Islands' in Europe at the time. While she did not enjoy Australia too much, her love for Hawaii spurred her to write her second book, after having climbed Mauna Kea and Mauna Loa.

After that, Isabella moved to Colorado because she had heard the 'air' was good there. In 1873 she took to horseback riding, and started a journey that would see her cover eight-hundred miles through the Rocky Mountains. She rode astride, facing forward, not side-saddle as most women did at the time. She was also noted for threatening to sue the English newspaper, *The Times*, when it said she looked like a man riding that way!

She wrote to her family every day, or as often as she could, and her letters from her Rocky Mountain expedition were printed in the *Leisure Hour* magazine, and they were also later compiled to form her book *A Lady's Life in the Rocky Mountains*.

Also during this expedition, she met Jim Nugent, AKA Rocky Mountain Jim, an outlaw with one eye and a love for violence and poetry, whom Isabella described as, "*A man any woman might love but no sane woman would marry.*"[2] Sadly, although their relationship was notable, he was shot dead just one year after she left the region.

Back home again, she met John Bishop, a young surgeon who would go on to propose to her. However, having read a piece by John Francis Campbell titled 'My Circular Notes, 1876', she decided she wanted to travel to and through Japan. And so, in 1878 she set off to travel through Japan, China, Korea, Vietnam, Singapore, and Malaya. During this time she got word that her sister Henrietta had passed from typhoid, in 1880. Sad and feeling it was the right thing to do, Isabella agreed then to marry John, in 1881.

The couple remained together until his passing in 1886. Although Isabella inherited a large amount of money, some of which was to be used to build a hospital, her health began to decline again, for she caught Scarlet Fever, a serious bacteriological infection. She did recover after some time, choosing then to study medicine and return to exploring and adventuring again, even though she was sixty years old by this time. She set off for India, where she would travel the land as a missionary.

In 1889 she worked a missionary in India, then in Ladakh in Tibet, then Persia, and Kurdistan, and Turkey. While in India, the Maharajah of Kashmir presented her with a piece of land, and Isabella decided it would be the perfect spot for the hospital John had wanted her to build. The hospital with sixty beds and a dispensary for women was duly built. With the help of her new friend, Fanny Jane Butler, the John Bishop Memorial Hospital went into action.

With the hospital functioning well, Isabella then accompanied a troupe of British soldiers on their travels between Baghdad and Tehran, arming herself with a revolver and a first-aid kit.

With this journey completed, she traveled further through Baluchistan to Persia and Armenia, along the Karun River. What she learned there would form the basis of a speech which she later gave in the British House of Commons on the persecution of Christians in Kurdistan.

With many journalists following her movements, she soon became well-known by people all over the world. In 1892, Isabella became the first woman to join The Royal Geographical Society. Never before had a woman been allowed a position within this revered Society.

Her final journey, in 1897, saw her travel alongside the Yangtze and Han Rivers in China and Korea, and then on to Morocco through the Atlas Mountains. There, she was gifted a magnificent black stallion by the Sultan. Just a few months after returning home from Morocco, Isabella fell ill at her home, 16 Melville Street, Edinburgh, and passed on October 7th, 1904, at the age of seventy-two.

Isabella was buried alongside her family members at the Dean Cemetery, west of the city. Pat Barr, a female British author, spoke of her as, "*One of the most popular, respected, and celebrated travelers of the later nineteenth century.*"[3]

What Urged Isabella to Choose the Path of Adventure?

Much like Gertrude Ederle, who also accomplished much despite her disabilities, Isabella was a woman who chose to challenge her own circumstances. She would not allow her pain and discomfort to take control of her life. Instead, she was determined to push through the worst and live a 'normal' life, if not one that exceeded others in the field of adventure.

Not many women are born with the kind of fire and passion needed to become an adventurer. Many are happy to remain housewives and raise children, while earning a small income. But for Isabella, the quiet life would not have been bearable, something she knew all too well from having been forced to spend a lot of time ill in bed with pain from spinal complications.

It is possible she developed insomnia as a way to prevent herself from feeling pain; it often happens that people with severe pain remain awake and get little sleep because they feel the need to stay on top of their pain. This can seem like a way to have control over it rather than the other way around. One can imagine her thinking alone, 'I refuse to spend the rest of my life in pain and in bed—I will make something of my life, and I will use my character and determination to achieve all I need to.' Similar things happen to many people who have faced trauma and discomfort; they see something in life that is worth living for, and they make it their goal in life to experience as many things as possible, simply so they can truthfully say, "I have lived."

Understanding a lot about local politics, religion, culture, and tradition from being raised in an environment where her father was often insulted for his beliefs, she likely became knowledgeable in these areas by overhearing people talking about them. Wanting to understand the differences between men and the various cultures, we can imagine how she would have listened with intent, possibly already determined to try to make a positive difference in the lives of others in her future.

She would have had a sincere interest in other cultures as a way to find humane common ground, a place where folks from all walks of life could meet at a point of mutual understanding in our world. Having been ill in her childhood and throughout most of her life, she would, no doubt, have seen 'togetherness' as being an important ingredient to humanity's success. She had plenty of personal experience about what it's like to be alone and unable to do things in the same ways others do, and she transferred that understanding to others.

She was dedicated to helping others, something which is borne out by every expedition she made, and through her opening and funding various hospitals. She also would have needed to be both greatly respectful as well as self-assured, so as to gain respect from the men and other authorities she met on her journeys.

While she had a curious, questioning mind as a child, as an adult woman she would have needed to pay attention to her attitude and mannerisms to win respect from those, mainly men, from whom she sought help in her quest to gain a greater understanding of life.

She would have needed to be very brave too because of all the dangerous territories she ventured through. As mentioned earlier, it is known that she carried small revolver with her on her travels.

Isabella was also the kind of person who believed that what does not kill you only makes you stronger. She would have gained much experience through every adverse circumstance she found herself in, and she doubtless used both danger and challenge as a way to build her strength and confidence.

This can be seen in a line which she wrote after a near brush with death—*"I felt that a new era of my existence had begun."*[4]

How Would Isabella Have Prepared for Her Adventures?

While some may say Isabella was privileged and given all she needed to achieve what she did, these were ultimately not the sole factors that led to her success.

Besides needing to be educated and knowledgeable of other cultures and being aware of worldly issues like politics and tradition, she would also have had to gather as much information about her destinations as possible ahead of time. That way, she could prepare somewhat for what she might expect to face on her adventure. This meant studying different countries, their laws, and also their languages, to gain at least some kind of understanding of the various languages she would have to use to communicate her purpose on her travels. Secondly, she would have had to know enough to find supplies, shelter, and food for the journey.

While she had been raised to believe that fresh air was the answer to her health problems, she would have also had to take or have the means to source some medications. She, therefore, had to know her physical self well, so as to know when she was able to push through a physical task and when it was best to rest.

While she had faith, she understood that not everyone has the same faith, and that not everyone lives in accordance with the ways of her family and community. She would have needed to develop tolerance, patience, bravery, and intuition (so as to know when to step back or move onward).

Perhaps Isabella's most developed skill was in the field of writing. Of course, with each expedition she made, she would either write a full book about it or a series of articles. She evidently had excellent communication skills and was able to convey her stories effectively.

Isabella's actions and choices show how creative she was. While some folks perceive an 'artist' or 'creative' as being someone who can paint or draw or sculpt a magnificent piece out of marble, Isabella had the 'gift of the gab' and great writing skills. She was able to hold the attention of her readers in the same way as a wonderful painting or other work of art can. This would have required her to work on her writing skills from an early age, as she was to use this skill throughout her life as a way to portray her findings, message, and purpose.

As for the physical journeys she made, she had to have been highly organized and prepared for whatever came her way. For instance, it would have been necessary to ensure she always had enough food and water for her adventures, as well as protection and, most important of all, a map! In addition, she must have learned to be a great judge of character, so as to know who to trust upon meeting new people.

Isabella would also have learned to use her time wisely and pace herself. Endurance is key when traversing the kind of path she chose in life, and it would have been vital for her to know her limitations and boundaries. It would make little sense to rush out on an adventure and then quickly become tired at having made headway too fast.

She likely either mapped out achievable routes for each day, as a way to conserve her energy and health, or functioned at a pace which enabled her to accomplish small daily goals. It would not have been a case of simply setting off with no planning and seeing where the day took her. She was a planner and worked with her resources wisely.

What Legacy Has Isabella Left Behind?

Isabella became known worldwide for her brave travels and related writings. She gained much criticism, sometimes being called foolish for traversing territory that some men would not even dare to face. However, she also received compliments and support for being respectful, tenacious, and as intently focused on her goal as she was.

Some of her achievements include:

- Alongside Fanny Jane Butler, she founded the John Bishop Memorial Hospital in Srinagar (today's Kashmir).

- Isabella was the first woman to be added as a Fellow of the Royal Geographical Society.

- Isabella founded five hospitals in memory of her lost family members, including her husband, who had left a reasonable sum of money for her to accomplish these tasks.

- After marrying John Bishop in 1881, she was awarded

the Royal Order of Kapiolani by King Kalakaua of Hawaii.

- Two years before becoming a Fellow of the Royal Geographical Society, she was awarded an Honorary Fellowship of the Royal Scottish Geographical Society.

- In 1897, she was awarded membership of the Royal Photographic Society.

- In Morocco she was given a black stallion by the Sultan, which she needed a ladder to mount!

- Isabella funded the building of the Clock Tower in Tobermory.

- In 1982, Caryl Churchill featured Isabella in her play *To Girls*, where much of the dialogue spoken was written by Isabella herself.

- In 1985, Isabella was added to the Colorado Hall of Fame.

- Isabella was featured in a book titled *Writers on the Wonders of Geology*, published in 2006 by Trinity University Press. The book pays tribute to the geological features of Earth and how the writings of various individuals have helped to create scope in this field.

- She had a great impact on others during her journey to Japan as well and was featured as the main character in a novel titled, *Fushigi no Kuni no Bird,* or *Isabella Bird in Wonderland*, a Manga story published in a bilingual edition in 2018.

- In December of 2022, a TV program titled *Trailblazers* presented a documentary on her trip through the Rocky Mountains. The broadcasters Ruby Wax, Mel B, and

Emily Atack retraced Isabella's steps through Colorado. The episode was titled "A Rocky Mountain Road Trip."

Some of Isabella's books include:

- *Korea and her Neighbors*
- *Journeys in Persia and Kurdistan*
- *Among the Tibetans*
- *The English Woman in America*
- *The Golden Chersonese and the Way Thither*
- *Notes on Old Edinburgh*
- *Unbeaten Tracks in Japan*
- *A Lady's Life in the Rocky Mountains*
- *Six Months in the Sandwich Islands*
- *My First Travels in North America*

Isabella wrote and published over one-hundred-and-fifteen books during her life as an adventurer and writer. Her written contributions helped not only to change the outlines of geographical maps of the world, but also the perceptions of folks across the globe regarding the different cultures, traditions, people, lifestyles, landscapes, and beliefs to be found in foreign countries.

Maria Spelterini

1853 - 1912

Who was Maria?

Maria Spelterini, sometimes referred to as 'Marie' was born in Livorno, Italy, on July 7th, 1853. With her father owning a traveling circus, she began performing with her family at the age of three. While she began with small acts, she grew to attempt new daring feats, and it was not long before she found her niche. This niche was tightrope-walking, and she would perform it across a body of water. The more treacherous the waters, the more appealing the attempt to cross it on a tightrope became to Maria.

Being a successful and much-loved funambulist (the professional term for tightrope walkers), she began touring Europe, and eventually joined a small club of Tightrope Daredevils. Her first major adventure was crossing the Moskva River in Moscow.

After that, she left people in awe as she crossed the River Neva in St. Petersburg. Then, in August of 1872, she crossed the Saint Aubin Harbor on the Island of Jersey, which was followed by her daring crossing at Catalan in August of 1873.

In 1876, Maria arrived in New York, where she continued to perform at the Jones Wood Coliseum. Her stunts included running backwards as well as seating herself on a chair on the wire, while remaining balanced for a period of time.

What made her unique, besides her obvious daring and adventurous spirit, was her choice of outfits for her shows. Weighing 150lbs at age twenty-three, she only ever performed in colorful outfits such as a scarlet tunic with a green bodice and smart 'buskin' boots. Most images of her available at this time are in black and white, although the creativity behind her outfits can still clearly be seen in these images.

Folks in the US and around the world were mesmerized by her bravery, focus, and happy persona. It was not long before she was being asked to perform at various national events, keeping audiences spellbound and on the edge of their seats.

Perhaps one of the most important events, not only for the US but also for her career, was the 1876 celebrations of the US Centennial, July 4th, which took place at Niagara Falls, New York. Her 2.1/4-inch wire was stretched across the wide gorge below the Railway Suspension Bridge (where Whirlpool Rapids Bridge is found today).

During the festivities, Maria performed five times in just one week, and these were the acts which led to her becoming world-famous. It is important to remember that a number of tightrope walkers had attempted the same act, notably the famed tightrope artist the Great Blondin in both 1859 and 1860, but Maria was the first woman to attempt and succeed in each crossing.

On July 8th, she crossed publicly for the first time. Determined to add more excitement to the show, she then crossed a second time on July 12th, but this time did so with peach baskets strapped to her feet, making it more difficult to remain balanced and find secure footing. Winning awe from the crowds, she then attempted a third show, this time crossing blindfolded with a paper-bag over her head. Her fourth attempt on July 22nd saw her crossing the gorge with her wrists and ankles in chains. For her fifth attempt, she crossed along the rope backwards without looking back, after which she proceeded to skip along the wire. After these shows at Niagara Falls, she went on to perform at the Centennial Exhibition in Philadelphia.

Maria never aimed to race time in her acts, however, choosing rather to complete the task successfully instead of risking imbalance through chasing a stopwatch.

Maria then took her act one step further and learned to ride a bicycle across a tightrope as well. In May of 1877, she readied herself for her attempt to cross in Rosario, Argentine, on her velocipede (another word for bicycle), but it malfunctioned on the wire itself and led to her first major public fall.

She survived, but this act was to be one of her last performances in public. After it, she stepped out of the public spotlight, and very little is known about where she went from there.

After having gained much attention, with newspapers like the *New York Herald* referring to her as '*gifted with wonderful nerve combined with cool daring*'[5], it is assumed she retired. But her legacy as one of the greatest performers in the world certainly still lives on today.

While her date of death was recorded as October 19th, 1912, the cause of her death was never publicly noted.

What Urged Maria to Choose the Path of Adventure?

Maria was raised in a family of circus performers, with her father owning a traveling circus. Her life began in the circus, and most of what influenced her would have come from the livelihood her family pursued.

It was likely an exciting life, and because performers are known to be determined and focused on bettering their own acts, she would have been around others who were always trying to better themselves as well. This form of motivation was likely what spurred her to attempt new feats, watching others bettering themselves and always perfecting their acts.

It would not have been a laid-back lifestyle, either, because in circuses, the whole crew work together as a team of extended family.

This is not to say it was obvious that she would have chosen also to become a performer. There are cases where youngsters do not find enjoyment in the paths their family follows, and they break away to do other things with their lives. However, she likely received a great deal of support and encouragement, and praise as well, when she performed her acts correctly or better than expected. These positively reinforcing moments were probably what helped her to achieve the courage and confidence she had.

But it is one thing to simply be good at something compared to being the first at something. Maria went on to be the first and only woman to cross Niagara Falls on a tightrope, an endeavor many would turn away from in fear of fatal injury.

She would have trained night and day and would have accepted her failures only to see them as 'points' to improve on in her performances. It is true that if someone is good at something they should pursue it and attempt to make it their source of stability and sufficiency, which is what she did. But beyond that, she would have also been passionate about 'being the first' to step outside of a physical comfort zone, in order to push her body to the limits to achieve her goals.

She was a remarkable entertainer and loved to dress up for her performances. She loved bright colors and enjoyed the attention from spectators. Traveling to various destinations with her Daredevil Club would doubtless have been exciting; she would have gotten to meet new people and experience new environments. Both are aspects of an adventurous lifestyle, where one is always wanting to try new things in order to truly feel one is living life to the fullest.

She would have needed to push herself onward in order to be the 'first' at a specific act, knowing she was the only one who would be able to take herself to new heights; no one else could get her there because her performance was centered on her personal abilities.

How Would Maria Have Prepared for Her Adventures?

At first, Maria traveled with her family and performed at various venues and events with them. After that, as she got older, she found a club to work with, a club that focused solely on the same niche of performance as her. Of course, balancing acts are a very specific form of art, and what better way to exist than with those who understand all you are doing, feeling, and saying?

It was likely difficult for her to step away from the security of her family, but she would have known the others in her club well before doing so. It seems likely they would have planned their trips to various locations together and funded them jointly too.

Maria would have needed to remain very fit and healthy in order to remain at her peak. It would have been necessary to keep her muscles flexible and strong, and she possibly practiced some form of meditation to keep herself calm and relaxed before performances.

The club would also have had to ensure it had enough funding for the performers to move from one venue to the next, which meant living within their means, meeting their day to day needs without spending lavishly.

For her performances, Maria would have had to maintain faith in herself and her ability to complete her acts without incurring injury. Any element of doubt would have led to an amount of fear creeping in, which might ultimately have prevented her from maintaining her balance or being focused enough to walk the thin line.

She would have had to remain emotionally strong and confident in herself, which likely was not too difficult, as she received a great deal of support from onlookers and fans.

And so, much like an athlete prepares for an event at the Olympics, she needed the same dedication to her art; she would have trained just as hard to be not only the best she could be, but also the best at her art. On the list of characteristics required to be a true adventurer, she ticks all the boxes.

What Legacy Has Maria Left Behind?

Maria will always be remembered for being the first (and only) woman to cross Niagara Falls five times in different ways. But besides her achievements, she left warmth and awe in the hearts of those she met. She was noted as being a 'breath of fresh air,' and she left those who saw her acts mind-boggled at what the human body can achieve in conjunction with the mind.

Thousands of people traveled to watch her performances at Niagara Falls, surely, a sight none could ever forget, leaving them with stories to tell about the amazing artist whom they saw defy gravity. On one occasion, she requested permission to cross the Brooklyn Bridge, which she was prepared for despite knowing it could lead to her death. However, the request was denied. She was never afraid to do new things, not because she had a net and security, but rather because she trusted her own abilities and instincts.

Most importantly, though, Maria left behind a legacy for women. In a world where men were seen as stronger, she demonstrated that agility, focus, and a lack of fear of danger were also equally important attributes. She showed that without these qualities, even the strongest man in the world would not have been able to come close to the acts she attempted and succeeded in.

She is also noted for being the figure who defined the "Year of the Woman" in a time when most woman were seen as only fit for the kitchen, motherhood, or shop, nursing, or secretarial positions. She promoted the aspect of adventure and thrill-seeking throughout her life, becoming a role-model to many adventurers around the world due to her tenacity.

A local paper, the *Niagara Falls NY Gazette*, at the time of her fame referred to her endeavors as *'traveling the gossamer web with a graceful, confident step, which soon allayed all apprehension of an impending disaster.'* [6]

Sherman Zavitz, a journalist from the local *Niagara Note* newspaper stated in an article about Maria that, *'Not only did she prove herself equal to her male predecessors on the rope, but she also undoubtedly also struck a blow for the equality of women.'*[7]

Although the second half of her life remains a mystery, as she dropped out of public sight after her major performances, she remains a legend. Perhaps she felt she had done enough, and that being the first and only to woman to cross Niagara Falls was a worthy legacy to leave behind.

After all, it's not always compulsory to set new goals once an adventurer feels they have attained self-fulfillment through achieving their most prized goal.

Hélène de Pourtalès

1868 - 1945

Who was Hélène?

Hélène de Pourtalès was born in New York City to Henry and Mary Barbey, on April 28th, 1868. Henry was a Swiss banker and financier and the director of the Buffalo, Rochester, and Pittsburgh Railway, and Mary's family owned the Lorillard Tobacco Company.

During the summers, the Barbey family would travel to Bellevue, Switzerland, where their favorite hobby was yachting. Hélène held dual citizenship, so she was able to travel freely between the United States and Switzerland. Henry preferred Hélène to spend as much time as possible in Switzerland, namely on Lake Geneva, as he believed the clean, healthy environment was far better for her than living in the smoke-filled city in the United States.

Being friends with Baroness Julie von Rothschild, a strong woman who also loved steam-boating and aimed to break existing speed records in boating, Hélène looked up to her friend. She saw Julie as a mentor in the area of boating, although she herself preferred sailing-boats to steamers.

Hélène's life was grand as she grew-up, for her parents were wealthy, influential, and respected members of their community, especially the Newport community, where

America's regattas were held during that era. In her diaries, Hélène wrote expressively on what she observed and learned during these regattas. She also loved horse-riding, a passion she developed due to her father's involvement in the British Derbies, where he was the American owner of the winning horse, Iroquois.

In 1891, Hélène was twenty-three-years-old. This was the year she met Hermann Alexander, Count de Pourtalès, who already had one son from his previous marriage, Guy de Pourtalès. They were married and went on to have three daughters of their own. Hermann was the captain of the Cuirassiers de la Garde regiment in the Prussian army. Once married, they began to compete in regattas together.

After a number of wins in local regattas in 1900, with the Olympics to be held in Paris, Hermann and Hélène decided to enter as a team. As part of the 1900 World's Fair, women would be allowed to compete in the Olympics for the first time in history. Of the 997 participants, only twenty-two were women. The events for women included golf, tennis, sailing, croquet, and equestrianism.

Because Hélène held dual citizenship, she was able to sail under the Swiss flag. She was thirty-two-years-old when the event took place. On May 22^{nd,} 1900, with twenty-two female competitors also striving for gold, she, along with her husband and nephew, sailed in the 1-2-ton Class race on their 20-foot boat, *Lerina*. The course was nineteen kilometers long and was considered to be one of the most technically challenging. The three-crew team won gold in their first race and silver in their second, with Hélène as skipper.

This is what made Hélène the first woman to not only participate in the Olympics sailing event, but also the first to win a gold medal. Because certain individuals did not think it was a woman's place to partake in the Olympics, Hélène (and other female competitors in other sporting categories) did not receive much praise or attention.

However, the title of *first woman* to take part in the Olympics as well as her gold medal can never be taken from her. She was certainly among the first few women to pave the way for women being able to participate in such major events.

In 1904, July 9th, Hermann passed away, leaving Hélène with roughly six-million US dollars. She went on to spend her time between Geneva and Paris, competing every so often, but no longer in world championship events.

While not much is known about her personal and family life after gaining her achievements, she is remembered worldwide for being the first woman to win a gold medal at the Olympics, as well as the first woman to represent Switzerland, thus winning the gold for Switzerland.

On November 2nd, 1945, at age seventy-seven, she passed away quietly at home in Geneva.

What Urged Hélène to Choose the Path of Adventure?

Hélène was raised in a family where partaking in sports was deemed as necessary as working. Her parents were very wealthy and influential, and this meant she was able, as a child, to observe her peers and learn from them. As she grew into a young woman, most of her life revolved around clothes, balls, galas, and other formal events, and handsome men who all held title in some or other field.

She was raised with respect and would have listened to her peers when they spoke, especially when she knew she was learning from the best.

With Geneva and its lake being so beautiful and perfectly suited for water sports, she developed a love for the waters in her younger years. It was this love for sailing that led her to focus on boating. While city life is preferred by some, she enjoyed the smell of the water and surrounding forests, and, of course, she was learning a new skill which, at the time, she did not realize would lead her to become the first woman to win an Olympic gold medal.

Perhaps she was also enthralled by the idea of being one of the first women to compete in the Olympics. She had support from her peers and family despite others disapproving of a woman participating in Olympic events.

She was surely given the opportunity to attend good schools and universities, but perhaps she wondered why women were discouraged from participating in competitive sports. Was she one of those women who challenged the status quo and dreamed of "breaking the glass ceiling"? She clearly felt that, for her, it was better to follow a sporting path, one which kept her healthy, invigorated, and feeling alive inside, while she battled the elements on a boat to show her strength, courage, and skill as a skipper.

It's important to note that being a skipper is similar to being the captain of a boat. It's the skipper's responsibility to command the boat, as well as take responsibility for the crew on board. They are also responsible for the functionality of the boat and its maintenance and upkeep.

In order to do this successfully, she would also have had to know a lot about how boats work. Of course, this was easy for her to learn because she had been raised in a boating family and community.

And so, it was Hélène's love for being on the open waters combined with a somewhat competitive spirit, as well as the opportunity of being one of the first women allowed to participate in the Olympics, that urged her toward the life of adventure she lived.

How Would Hélène Have Prepared for Her Adventures?

Not everyone enjoys sailing, and not everyone has the skill to sail a boat. Being a sailor requires specific training, but all of the necessary skills can be acquired if the individual has a deep passion for the sport and is not afraid of deep water.

Hélène would have developed her passion for boats through her family and their friends, for she frequently attended boating events with them. She would have learned to steer a boat, and also the names of boat parts, from an early age. And so, when we find no textbooks to teach us how to acquire certain skills, we **observe** our peers. As we observe, we find questions to ask that help to make things clear to us. We also learn through *doing* what our peers do in our given field. Observation would have been a method used by Hélène to learn as much as did about boats.

Training is not always the most fun part of any sport. Often, we have to train in conditions that are not favorable. For Hélène, an example if this would be if she needed to train to race in choppy, rough waters. She would have needed to know how to use her hands to ensure she gripped the ropes firmly and not let go. She would have learned how to position her body weight to ensure the boat remained balanced when necessary. And she would have had to be super-fit and strong to be able to keep her balance and handle the elements as they arose. And so, she would have been trained—most likely by her father—to do as he said in order to develop the skills she had.

Beyond the hands-on experience she had to accumulate, she would also have learned some **theory** about boats, mostly the names of the parts and terminology used in sailing. Her training would not have consisted only of physical exercise; there would also have been some theory involved too. It's likely she would have had to pass a few tests, even if only verbal ones, to ensure she at least knew port from starboard!

She certainly would have needed to develop patience for her sport, especially if she was sailing with a crew. She certainly would have had to learn how to be a fair 'leader.' **Patience** can be a very important quality in sport; Aesop's old fable *The Tortoise and the Hare* teaches us that winning is not always about being the fastest. Winning often depends on being focused, being able to endure, and pacing ourselves so as not to make mistakes or tire ourselves out to early.

Hélène would also have had to be very **confident** in her skills. Without this confidence, she might have made mistakes that would have shown her as incapable of being a skipper. At the time she entered the Olympics to compete, there were numerous men, and even women, who believed neither sailing nor the Olympic event itself were any place for a decent woman. Of course, in those times, most women were housewives or mothers, and other roles were scarce. But Hélène remained confident and continued along her path with blinkers on, so to speak, determined not be swayed by the nay-sayers. In truth, she would have been both confident in herself and in her skills as a boater.

She also would have required great **physical strength**. Trying to sail a boat in rough water against the winds and elements is not for the faint hearted, of course. She would have kept her body strong, and her muscles supple by following a **healthy** diet as well as through her daily exercises. In addition, she would have had to maintain good balance, which requires good **motor skills**.

Her ability to focus would have had to be strong as well, to constantly be aware of unforeseen hurdles, even before they arose. This would have made her attentive, strong, and **determined**, without a need to overtake or overthrow others. Her success shows she realized that good leadership requires an understanding of the importance of the team working together as whole, and not just the leader.

Overall, Hélène will always be remembered as a woman who paved the way for women to compete at the Olympics, and to eventually have their own categories in various sporting challenges. She was one of the pioneers who set the course for women to prove their worth across competitive sports.

What Legacy Has Hélène Left Behind?

Besides being remembered as adventurous and spirited, Hélène's main claim to fame is obviously that she was one of the first women (of twenty-two) to not only compete in the Olympics but also win gold in her class. She was also the first woman to represent Switzerland at the Olympics, and her victory was as much of a celebration for Switzerland as it was for her and her family.

Her most notable medals include a gold in the 1-2 Ton Open with her boat, *The Lerina 1*, as well as a silver in the 1-2 Ton Open with *Lerina 2* in 1900.

She was listed among the First Female Competitors at the Olympics by a country (Switzerland), and she was also listed in the Olympian Members of Nobility as a Countess.

Hélène was also recognized by the International Olympic Committee as one of the first Olympic champions in history, alongside Englishwoman Charlotte Reinagle Cooper, who won a gold medal in the sport of tennis in 1900, as well as American women Marion Jones and Hedwig Rosenbaum, who both won bronze medals in tennis.

Without women like Hélène, it is difficult to know just when women would have been allowed into, and eventually welcomed, the sphere of internationally competitive sports. She joins the small band of women from around the world whose determination made it possible for females to compete and win!

MISS LONDONDERRY.

Annie Londonderry

1870 - 1947

"I am a journalist and 'a new woman' if that term means that I believe I can do anything that any man can do." ~ Annie Londonderry

Who Was Annie?

While her exact date of birth is unknown, Annie Cohen Kopchovsky was born in 1870, in Latvia. Her parents were Levi and Beatrice Cohen. Two of her four siblings were born in Latvia, with the other two later being born in the United States.

When she was roughly four or five-years-old, in 1875, her family moved from Latvia to the United States as Jewish immigrants, eventually becoming citizens. They eventually settled in Boston, Massachusetts. Her father, Levi, passed away on January 7th, 1887, followed by her mother just two months later. By this time, Annie was seventeen-years-old. While her sister was married and living in Maine, Annie and Bennet, her twenty-year-old brother, raised their two younger siblings Jacob (who passed away due to a lung infection aged only seventeen) and Rosa.

Both Annie and her brother soon found partners of their own and were married. They lived as a large family together with their spouses and siblings in their Spring Street home in Boston.

Annie's husband was Simon 'Max' Kopchovsky. He was a 'peddler' selling second-hand clothes and household items, and he studied the Torah as an Orthodox Jew. Annie worked selling advertising space for a few daily Boston newspapers.

It so happened that, in 1894, when Annie was just twenty-four-years-old, a man living in Boston made a bet that no woman could travel around the world on a bicycle. The woman who could would receive $10,000 as a prize. After all, a journey like this had only ever been completed by a man, in 1885.

Annie had never really ridden a bicycle, and she was only given three months to prepare and plan for her adventure. She happily accepted the challenge, and on June 25th, she announced to a crowd of 5000 people at the Massachusetts State House that she intended to travel 'around the world on a bicycle.'

She would ideally become an example of how effective bicycles were as a form of transportation. She may have helped to popularize 'bloomers' as a form of women's bicycling clothing, for they were far more convenient to ride in than cumbersome skirts.

The initial rules of the bet were that she would begin her journey without any money at all. She would then have to earn at least $5000 over and above her travel expenses on the way, and she had to finish the trip in fifteen months. This was not to be a test of a woman's physical strength, rather it was a test to see a woman's ability to 'fend for herself' in the world. Indeed, Annie carried a pistol with her on her journey for protection.

Because of her experience in advertising through working with various Boston newspapers, her first sponsor was the Londonderry Lithia Spring Water Company of Nashua, New

Hampshire, who gave her $100 to display the company's logo on her 42-lb Columbia bicycle. And this was how she first became known as 'Annie Londonderry.'

She began her journey from Boston on June 25th, 1894, heading west to Chicago, where she was given a lighter bicycle and sponsorship from the Sterling Cycle Works. Next, she headed back to New York, where she boarded a ship to France.

There had been no specific rules regarding how she would cross oceans, so crossing by boat was allowed. However, even though she did not ride her bike on any roads while aboard the ship, she rode around the deck for a few hours each day so as still to be seen as 'cycling around the world.'

From France she travelled through Europe, Asia, and Japan, eventually arriving back in the United States, in San Francisco, California, on March 23rd, 1895. On one occasion, after cycling along the Santa Fe railroad track through New Mexico to Denver, she contracted pneumonia. She was bed-ridden for fourteen days, although these 'lost days' did not hinder her deadline for arrival at the end.

She also managed to ride straight into a drove of pigs at one stage, was chased by a horse, broke her arm, and spent time in a jail cell in China during the Sino-Japanese war. In her writings she claims that one of the officers killed another man 'right in-front of my eyes.' Whether or not such stories were actually true remains a mystery!

Her final trip led her back to Boston, where she arrived on September 24th, 1895, and was awarded the promised $10,000 in Chicago.

She certainly did finance her own adventure. From the day she left to embark on her adventure, she was featured in various newspapers worldwide and started earning more money by selling autographed photographs of herself on her bike. Some even referred to her as a 'travelling billboard,' considering the number of ribbons and cards she adorned herself and her bike with to advertise her sponsors.

It also turned out that Annie was an amazing storyteller. She would often exaggerate about her adventures and her accomplishments, and her stories were heard by all those who met her. Some of her exaggerations led to scandal (especially once it became known that she had covered a lot of the ground via train or ship) and doubts in her credibility. But those who understood she was all about 'adventure' and trying new things in life became fond of her and followed her travels through the various media available at the time.

Once she'd settled back at home in New York, she was awarded a writing job with a magazine called *New Woman*. Through her writings she would speak of her adventures while cycling around the world. At the time, she believed she had tamed the fiery adventurer within and returned to being a mother, raising her children to become successful and adventurous too!

Annie would go on to be well-known for her adventure and personality, although not quite as famous as a film star. The cause of her death was said to be a stroke. She passed on November 11th, 1947.

What Urged Annie to Choose the Path of Adventure?

Annie had grown up under difficult circumstances. She became a mother and wife at a very early age, and it seems likely that the main reason for accepting the challenge to ride around the world on a bicycle was because she needed relief from a life which gave her no freedom. On accomplishing her journey, she came out richer and better known, which would have helped her family in the long run. However, the offer of $10,000 prize money certainly would have encouraged her to accept the challenge.

Perhaps those who are kept in circumstances that make them feel constrained are naturally spurred into adventure, knowing there is much more to life than simply working to make ends meet and raising children.

Annie was very good at what she did with regards to advertising and public relations. Before her journey, she had also read numerous news stories daily about other people achieving great things. Of course, she soon decided she wanted to be one of them!

She had great self-esteem as well, and even if others did not like her, it's possible she simply believed they did not understand her. She did not do what she did for fame; she did it because it was fun. Because of her extrovert personality, she was able to promote herself and thus earn the money she needed to win the bet, and ultimately pay her way. In the long run, her efforts led to her and her family living a pretty good life once she returned from the trip. An example of her 'entrepreneurship' and self-promotion skills was her ability to earn an additional $3000 for simply giving a lecture about cycling en route.

She was occasionally referred to as a liar for embroidering her stories, although storytellers will understand that a little overdramatization of certain events can make them seem more exciting to listeners than they might otherwise be. Of course, she had her own feelings, so perhaps exaggerating was a way for her to express the experience to the fullest.

Being a mother, in those times deemed the most suitable role for women in society, and a working woman, she used her personality and achievement to alter this stereotype. By doing so, she helped the world see that women can be just as strong and self-sufficient as men when they put their minds and hearts into it.

Annie was able to live in a world of her own, without needing permission from others to act. Many of the stories she told sounded quite bizarre and unlikely, but this did not stop her. Those who followed her understood she was more of a traveling storyteller, exciting both young and old with her tales of adventure, even though there were a few that could not be proven to have taken place.

Indeed, she became one of the pioneers to spur women's equality in the world. She took part in hundreds of exhibitions during her journey, giving lectures and demonstrations on her bike. She was interviewed countless times, though some interviewers were stumped because she only spoke in English; some of the international press members could not understand her, although they evidently saw her daring quest and friendly personality as fresh, new, and exciting.

Overall, her life became fun, and each new day would bring fresh opportunities. An example of this was when she realized winter was coming and that she would not be able to reach her destination on her bike. Instead, she chose to veer off in the opposite direction, thus changing her initial plan to suit her environment, a sign of **adaptability**.

Annie was like a butterfly who finally took the opportunity to emerge from her cocoon and fly to heights neither she nor anyone else in her family had ever thought possible. She teaches us that opportunities should never be overlooked, that even if something sounds unachievable, even a little ridiculous, with good planning, self-confidence, and a passion for adventure, such opportunities can take us to new places, leaving us with stories to share forever.

How Did Annie Prepare for Her Adventures?

Perhaps the most important part of Annie's journey was that she had to accumulate her own funding. The two men who bet on whether or not a woman could ride around the world on a bicycle did not give her any money at all; the deal was that she would receive $10,00 only if she accomplished her task.

And so, what she would have focused on most during her preparations, and even through her entire journey, was her people-oriented personality and confidence. No one was going to give her anything unless she asked, and no one really ever gives money to anyone who is not confident in what they're doing.

She only had three months to prepare for the journey as well. In fact, it is said she did not even know how to ride a bicycle at first. So, she would have needed to train to not only cover enough ground per day, but also to keep her body fit and muscles at peak performance so as not to develop issues like cramp or even back pain.

She also helped to create bloomers, which were the puffy, baggy pants worn by women instead of dresses that simply were not bicycle-friendly! Although bicycles did not have too many components back in those days, she would also have needed to know how to maintain her bicycle for punctures or faulty pedals or crank-arms and such. She would have needed to know her bike as well as she knew herself, and this required training too.

She was a master storyteller as well, and this might not have been something she learned to do as much as something she wanted to do. It was said that her dare-devil-type stories were fictional, and that she only created them as ways to gain more publicity and sponsorship. Even if this was true, kudos to her for having an awesome imagination!

Once her journey was 'on the road,' she also received letters from the general public congratulating her for her achievements as well as urging her to complete the next leg of her journey. Not assuming fame, she would reply to each letter she received—not so much out of duty but mostly because she really enjoyed interacting with people.

Of course, there were a few times when she physically felt as though she could not continue her journey, an example being how she felt after covering 1,300-miles in three months. She had lost 20lbs, and was extremely tired, and was starting to feel weak. But she did not give up. She met her goal and achieved what she set out to, regardless of obstacles like physical health challenges that seemingly stood in her way.

What Legacy Has Annie Left Behind?

Although at the time Annie did not share the same fame as models, actors, or musicians, the mark she left in the world of women was profound.

Annie became a symbol of freedom, as did the invention, production, and use of the bicycle itself. During its introduction, the bicycle became seen as *'having done more to emancipate women than anything else in the world,'* [8] according to suffragist Susan B. Anthony.

The *Boston Evening Transcript* said this of her: "*Packing only a change of underwear and a pearl-handled revolver, Annie Londonderry sailed away like a kite down Beacon Street.*"[9]

A book written about her fantastic adventure, titled *Around the World on Two Wheels: Annie Londonderry's Extraordinary Ride* was written by Peter Zheutlin (Annie's great nephew). It details her adventure from start to finish. Peter explains her personality well, describing her as *'brash, outlandish, and charismatic.'* He also called her a *'master self-promoter and creator of her own myth.'*

In 2011 Evalyn Parry produced a bicycle-themed performance based on Annie's journey that claimed much attention. A review by *The Southern Bookseller* magazine describes it thus: "*The reader gets to ride along with Annie as she meets the most famous people of the day and finds love and adventure in every long mile.*"[10]

In Evalyn's performance, which was presented on her tour through Canada and the USA, she featured a song called 'The Ballad of Annie Londonderry.'

A writer and film-director from Spokeswoman Productions, named Gillian Klempner Willman, also went on to create a 26-minute documentary about Annie's life and journey. It was titled *The New Woman—Annie Londonderry Kopchovsky*, and it premiered at the DC Independent Film Festival in 2013. It won the award for Best Documentary.

It is apparent that Annie's legacy still lives on—as can be seen in the musical production starring Liv Andrusier and Yuki Sutton that was performed at the Charing Cross Theater as recently as 2022.

Of course, Annie received much backlash about her tales of adventure, with some folks even claiming there had never been any bet at all. It was suggested that she had made up the whole idea as a way to escape the responsibilities of motherhood and live a life of fantasy.

Fortunately, such people were in a minority. Many more loved Annie for her sparky character, endurance, and ability to enthrall with her entertaining tales of her travels. Few paid much attention to those who did not see the magic she was able to create through her life, especially in the hearts of those who were unable to embark on such adventures.

In the *New York World* magazine, writers claimed that hers was '*the most extraordinary journey undertaken by a woman.*'[11]

Just as Walt Disney set out to appeal to young women in finding the perfect soulmate, or Prince Charming, Annie set out to create a 'story' for others, to inspire them with a zest for life, travel, and adventure. However, her journey was very real—film footage of riding her bike through all the different locations still exists—and it boggles the mind to imagine some of strange and occasionally perilous situations she must have faced along the way. Who can blame her for a little exaggeration now and then?

It's clear Annie understood that any adventure tale needs a few added touches in the telling, to highlight the exciting parts, to make it sound fantastic, daring, and magical—just like her incredible bicycle ride 'around the world'!

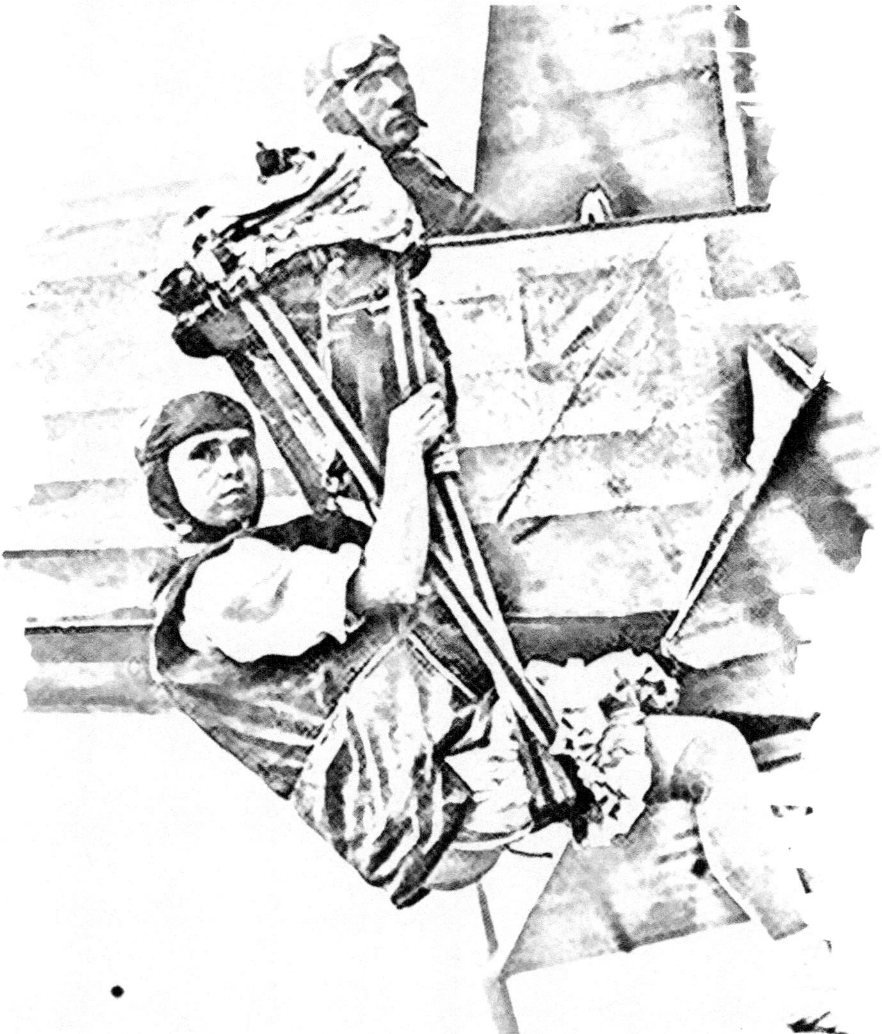

Tiny Broadwick

1893 - 1978

"When I saw that balloon go up, and I gawked at it as it ascended into the heavens, I knew I'd never be the same."
~ Tiny Broadwick

Who was Tiny?

Georgia Ann 'Tiny' Thompson Broadwick was born to George and Emma Ross on their farm in Oxford, Granville County, North Carolina, on April 8th, 1893. She was the seventh daughter born to the Ross's and was given the nickname 'Tiny' because she was so small. It is noted that even as an adult she was only 5 feet tall and weighed in at 36kg (80lbs). Hence her nickname, which stuck with her throughout her life.

Tiny spent her early years on the farm with her parents and sisters. They struggled to make money, however, and so the family moved to Henderson, where Tiny's father began working at the local cotton-mill.

In those days it happened often that young girls would marry very young, perhaps as a way to lighten the load of family responsibilities. And so Tiny was married in 1905 at the very young age of just twelve. The following year she fell pregnant and gave birth to a daughter, Verla. The name of her first husband has never been clear, but within a year of them being parents, he abandoned them, leaving Tiny to raise Verla on her own. Tiny continued to work in the cotton-fields as before, but by age fifteen, she was struggling to keep things together.

At around this time, she happened to see a performance by Charles Broadwick's World Famous Aeronauts. They jumped out of a hot-air balloon with parachutes, a stunt that drew crowds from across the region. She was thrilled by what she saw. After the performance, she sought Charles Broadwick out, telling him, "*I knew that's all I ever wanted to do.*"[12]

It was decided that she would join their traveling team. While some thought they were married, it was rather that Charles 'adopted' Tiny—hence her new surname, Broadwick. Tiny's daughter Verla was then raised by Tiny's parents, with Tiny sending them money as often as she could for her upkeep.

Charles took advantage of her small size and created a character for her, 'Doll Girl.' He dressed her in ruffled bloomers, a silk dress, put ribbons in her ringlets, topped off nicely with a bonnet. Although Tiny did not like the character she played, nor the outfit she was asked to wear, she soon became the star of the show and the 'sweetheart' of the carnival crowds.

Tiny was only fifteen when she jumped from a hot-air balloon for the first time, in 1908, on December 28th, at the North Carolina State Fair. She described her feelings about this first jump, stating, "*I tell you, honey, it was the most wonderful sensation in the world.*"[13] Tiny would go on to perform over one-thousand jumps before the end of her career.

She was determined and seldom deterred by falls and accidents. Although she experienced several life-threatening scenarios, such as landing on the caboose of a train, getting tangled-up in a windmill and tension wires, and breaking or dislocating bones, she never lost her love for the jump.

While she had only ever jumped from hot-air balloons, she and Charles attended a Los Angeles Air Met where they met stunt-flyer and airplane manufacturer Glenn L. Martin. He asked Tiny to be the first woman to jump from a real aircraft.

And so, Tiny became the first woman to parachute from an airplane on June 12th, 1913. Her parachute had been made by Charles, and the jump started out with her hanging from a trapeze-like swing beneath and just behind the wing of Martin's airplane. At 2000-feet, she released the cord and gracefully floated back down to the ground, landing in Griffith Park. This, of course, won her world acclaim.

In 1914 she became the first woman to parachute over a body of water, namely Lake Michigan. After a few more daring jumps, during World War I, the US Army soon heard about her and her skills, and contacted her to assist them in training their soldiers and men on how to jump from a plane successfully. She would demonstrate the jump four times, with the first three jumps being successful, but the fourth a little more complicated.

It had always been with parachuting that the parachute itself would be attached to the moving airplane, released only by the jumper pulling a small lever. However, during her fourth demonstration at San Diego's North Island, the wind caused complications, and she found herself having to cut the line short and freefall to the ground, pulling the line to open the chute by hand.

This was seen as a remarkable occurrence, and it was noted as the very first free-fall descent. It paved the way for the invention of the 'rip cord,' and also gave confidence to other flyers that pilots and jumpers could now jump from a failing plane without falling to their death. As a small woman, she was the first person to prove this was possible, and this is seen as one of her most profound contributions to the world of parachuting and aviation.

It is a story that will be told by parachutists for years to come, as she actually invented the 'rip cord' purely by accident, after using her logic to ensure she did not die from the fall.

Tiny would eventually break away from Charles, but kept the Broadwick name for her performances. She went on to jump for two more years, between 1920 and 1922. But in 1922, at the age of twenty-nine, she was urged to retire after suffering with problems in her ankles.

She received much recognition for her acts, and although she was not a pilot by any means, she was one of the few female members of the Early Birds of Aviation, an organization dedicated to the history of early pilots, established in 1928. One of her more well-known quotes was: *"I breathe so much better up there, and it's so peaceful being that near to God."*[14]

With regards to her personal life, while Tiny was traveling with the troupe, she married Andrew Olsen in 1912. Their relationship did not stand the test of time, however, and so when she met Harry Brown and they got along well, she married him. Hence, she kept the name Georgia Brown. Sadly, this marriage did not work out either.

After a strong and meaningful career, Tiny spent the last of her years in California before passing on in 1978 at the age of eighty-five. Because Henderson was where it had all begun for her, her body was buried in Henderson, North Carolina, where her legacy still lives on today.

What Urged Tiny to Choose the Path of Adventure?

Tiny was born to a less fortunate family and was one of seven children, all girls, in the family. After her father moved them to Henderson, there were likely financial demands they struggled to meet. In those days, sending daughters out young to be married meant there would be less of a financial burden on the family. This is what happened to Tiny at only twelve-years-old. She then gave birth at age thirteen, which today means she would be regarded as a child. Being forced to give birth at such a young age would be deemed a violation against her Human Rights.

After her first husband abandoned her and Verla, she had to go to work in the cotton-fields as well, at around age fourteen. She never had the opportunity to live a normal life like many other kids. So, when she saw opportunity knocking, she took the chance, perhaps feeling that the risk of falling to her death from a hot-air balloon was worth taking when compared to her hard life. However, she clearly understood that if she succeeded, it would be a great life full of fun and adventure. In short, she had nothing to lose when she joined Charles Broadwick and his troupe, and was more than willing to take the risk.

It is said that in times of trouble we look up to the sky, and perhaps even wish for someone to reach down and pull us out of our troubles. It could be said that this is what happened to Tiny, and she lived a fruitful life afterwards, due to her bravery and 'all or nothing' character.

She explains through numerous interviews that when she first flew and then ultimately made her first jump, she felt better than she ever had before. The experience gave her a new perspective on life; it filled her with vitality and a zest for living that would have seen her wake each day to the promise of some new, thrilling adventure.

It's likely that because she was forced into making life-changing choices at such a young age, she naturally became a practical, logical thinker and good at problem solving, what with having to fend for herself at just about every turn.

Being in the clouds among the birds, living a life of danger that would always be rewarded on achieving success, was one she felt was worth living. She got to meet a lot of exciting people, and even received recognition from various authorities, as well as the US Army, for whom she went to work as a demonstrator.

It's not to say that Tiny was born with the desire to jump from parachutes or fly in an airplane. Rather, it was that she was at an extremely low point in her life. In fact, she'd likely never known many high points when she attended the airshow headed by Charles Broadwick. Her dreamer spirit may have kicked in, allowing her to believe she could become an Aeronaut as well. After all, why not? One either fails—or in her case, falls—or succeeds; it must have seemed to her that she had few other choices or opportunities to escape the difficult circumstances she found herself in at just aged fourteen.

Had she not found any thrill in her first jump, it's unlikely she would have continued with it. But she certainly was one of the few in life who find themselves presented with a life-changing opportunity, and she did well to take it. She loved her life and what she did, and this is clear in that she always returned to the skies, even after falls that left her with broken bones.

A lucky 'Girl Doll' she was at the start! But beyond that, to have served the US Army in the war effort was an honor she could never have expected, especially considering she was a woman teaching men how to jump. This would have given her greater self-esteem as well, and confidence in herself, as opposed to merely living for the thrill-screams of anxious onlookers.

How Would Tiny Have Prepared for Her Adventures?

Being small was Tiny's secret weapon and the key to her being able to do what she did so often and so successfully. Having come from a less fortunate family unable to raise her to become self-sufficient and confident and being unable to pursue any kind of career because she had to raise her daughter, she had no other deep commitments to hold her back. While being a mother is obviously important, by modern standards, being a mother at age thirteen is unacceptable.

Once she got going and it was discovered how good she was at what she did, she would have moved with the troupe. It's certain the performers would have had their own routines each day, to ensure they remained healthy and strong, both physically and mentally.

She might not have needed to work on psychological preparation as much as others because of her 'all or nothing' mindset; she already knew there was not much else to live for.

She would also have needed to learn to remain calm to some degree, as panicking while in mid-air has never proved to help anyone in the aeronaut industry! She likely meditated in some way before performances, or 'had a quiet word with God,' asking that should she fall, the end be quick and painless. She would have needed to work on her breathing not only to remain calm, but also to handle the air-pressure at such great heights. Short breaths deplete oxygen to the brain, whereas longer, more concentrated breaths ensure the body functions at its optimum capacity.

She would have developed superior focus as well, especially under the conditions she faced while hanging from an airplane. To be able to remember each step that needs to be taken, and to remain calm while doing so, would have been extremely important. Her power of concentration was certainly proven during her free-fall fourth jump. To be able to find a solution under such dramatic circumstances shows she was self-reliant, clearly knowing that no one but herself could help her out of her situation.

Having an excellent knowledge of planes and parachuting equipment would have been essential too. Had she not done her homework in this area of her career, it is unlikely she would have made the lightning-quick decision she did on that fourth jump, where she 'by accident' (and excellent judgement) was able to cut her own cord, basically inventing the ripcord and taking aeronautics to new heights.

She would have needed to be fast healer as well, in the sense that when she had a fall and was injured, she recovered quickly, thanks probably to a healthy diet and general physical fitness. This helped her to continue performing.

For Tiny, it seems likely that the daredevil spirit which obviously fueled her was born from lack of choice. When we are faced with a life that seems too difficult to live, which drains us each day, and leaves us with no hope for the future, we welcome adventure and a chance to tackle new and exciting challenges.

What Legacy Has Tiny Left Behind?

Tiny will always be remembered as one of the greats in aviation and parachuting. Given the title 'First Lady of Parachuting,' her name will always be in the textbooks and acknowledgements in this regard.

Some of the recognition she received (according earlyaviators.com) includes:

1. Having a portion of the Henderson Outer Loop Highway, in Vance County, North Carolina, named after her in 2006.

2. Having a street in Rancho Dominguez, California, named after her, namely Broadwick Street.

3. Appreciated in 1964 for her donation of a parachute handmade by Charles Broadwick, which consisted of 110-yards of silk, to the Smithsonian Air Museum, the precursor to the Smithsonian Air and Space museum.

4. Receiving the US Government Pioneer Aviation Award, as well as a John Glen Medal (John Glenn was the first American ever to orbit the Earth).

5. Tiny was one of the first women to become a member of the Early Birds of Aviation, and also received the 'Gold Wings' of the Adventurer's Club in Los Angeles.

6. In 1964, Tiny became an honorary member of the 82nd Airborne Division at Ft. Bragg and was told she would have the privilege of being able to jump with them at any time.

7. In 1961, January 20th became known as Tiny Broadwick Day in Henderson, North Carolina. On that day, Tiny was awarded a plaque in recognition of her efforts in parachuting.

The plaque states:

"Presented to Tiny Broadwick by Commander, Group VII and Henderson Squadron, Civil Air Patrol; known for her contribution to the development of aviation and her accomplishments with the parachute; she will rank with the pioneers in the field of early aviation." [15]

8. Tiny also appeared on many TV shows, including 'You Bet Your Life' (1955); 'To Tell The Truth' (1964); and 'Mysteries at the Museum' (Season 11).

Some of the more special awards and honors she received include:

- Awarded by the Survival and Flight Equipment Association (By Bob Snider, President).

- Awarded by the OX5 Club (by Harlan A. Gurney, President, Southern California Wing).

- Awarded by The Early Birds of Aviation, Inc. (by Forrest E. Wysong, Secretary).

- Awarded by the United States Parachute Association (by Norman Heaton, Executive Director).

It is said that 'dynamite comes in small packages,' and Tiny certainly proved this to be right. From starting out in what seemed like a dead-end life, she chose to throw caution to the wind in search of a new life that she could live feeling fulfilled and worthy.

She shows us that anything is possible when we are prepared to let go of the mundane, in order to search for the life we want, the life we have the right to live. This life is one filled with new experiences and adventures that serve to make us realize just how strong we really are—despite what others may previously have thought.

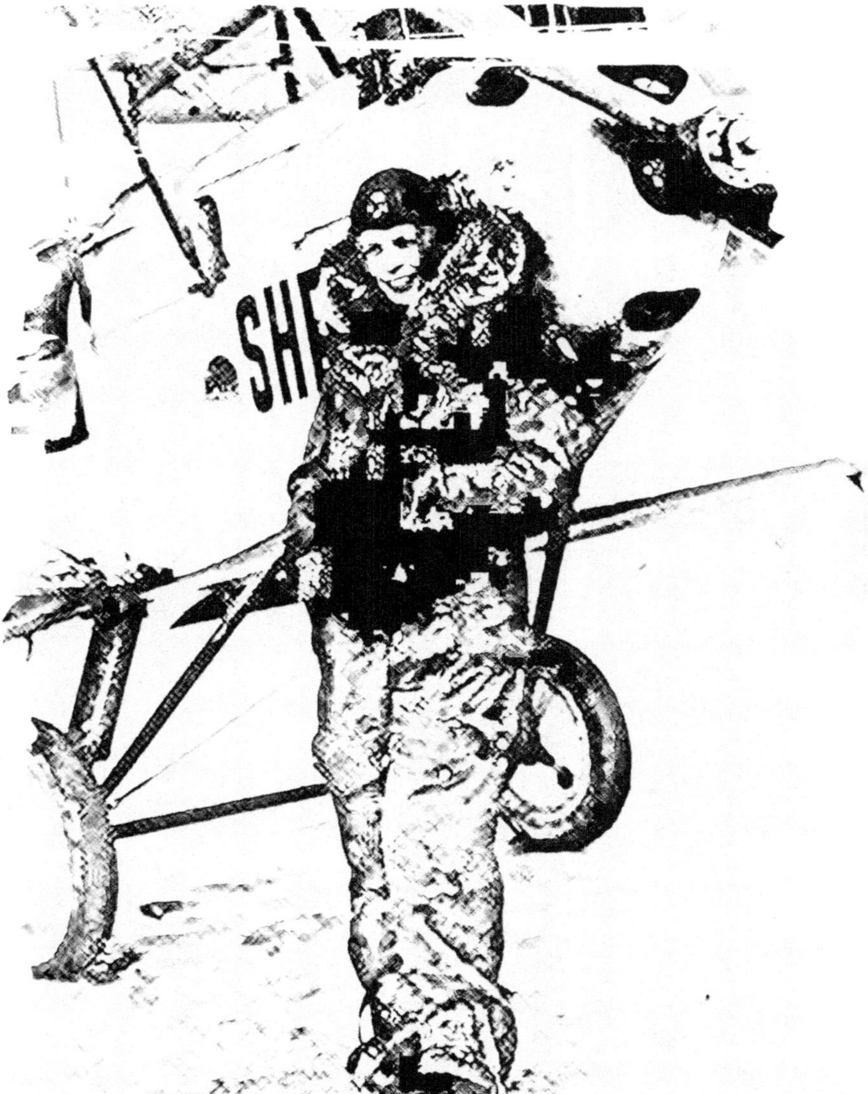

Eva Dickson

1905 - 1938

Who was Eva?

Eva was born Eva Lindstrom in southern Sweden, in Sigtuna, on March 8[th,] 1905. Her father, Albert Lindstrom, managed a few stud farms along with his wife, Maria. It was a very profitable business. Albert was an author of several books about horse-breeding, and Eva naturally developed a love of horse-riding.

When she was in her early teens, Eva's family moved to Ljung, near Linkoping, where Eva was raised in a real castle, namely Ljung Castle. She was home-schooled there, learning subjects like math, writing, Christian Studies, and drawing. In 1916 her father was employed as director-in-chief for the Stockholm Stud. Once again, her family moved and settled, this time in Stockholm. Eva then began attending school, firstly Brummer School, and then Anna Sandstrom School.

Eva had an older brother named Ake. Their childhood together was wild and filled with mischief and exploration, as well as dining in fancy restaurants and attending the social events held by the elite associates of her parents.

By her late teens, she was already moving in circles with wealthy, influential people, and she soon met rally driver Olaf Dickson. They became good friends, and by the time Eva turned twenty in 1925, they were married. They lived a life of exploration and adventure, traveling through Europe by car and motorcycle, while Olaf taught Eva all she needed to know about rally-driving.

In 1927, Eva entered her first major rally event, which would lead to her competing in numerous rallies thereafter. However, some of these rally events were for males only, and so she would register herself under the name Anton Johansson and pretend to be a man. She did very well at rally-driving and would finish most of the events in the top ten of competitors.

Of course, her driving skills and extroverted yet mischievous personality soon led to her gathering a following. Because she had studied and enjoyed writing, she began to record her travel adventures in a journal her and would go on to publish travel guides which included tales of her personal experiences behind the wheel.

Her travels obviously required funding, though, and she was not the type to expect others to pay her way. And so, she would make bets with wealthy members of society, using her winnings to cover her expenses. The more popularity she gained, the further she could travel. However, eventually, Olaf became unhappy about her traveling all the time, and so they were divorced in 1932.

Eva then met Baron Bror von Blixen-Finecke in Kenya. He had previously been married to the author of a world-famous book titled *Out of Africa*, Karen Blixen. They began a new relationship together, and both had a passion for traveling, tours, and going on safari in Africa. Not only did they have common interests, but also Eva's brother Ake and Bror were good friends.

At this time, still in 1932, Eva made a bet that she could cross the Sahara from Nairobi to Stockholm by car. She certainly achieved what she set out to and became the first woman to do so in history.

A Kenyan friend, Hassan Ali, accompanied her on the journey, which took twenty-seven days to complete. She drove an open four-seater Chevrolet equipped with water bags, oil drums, spare parts, petrol, and cooking equipment. It was no easy journey at all, and Eva suffered from malaria for around forty days.

On arrival back in Sweden she was greeted and welcomed by the Royal Automobile Club. This, of course, gained her much attention worldwide, and interest in her written travel guides grew immensely; others wanted to know more about this little woman who drove through the desert on a bet. By 1933, her guides were highly sought after, which only spurred her to want to travel further and write more.

In 1934, she returned to Kenya with Bror. Together, they embarked on a number of scientific expeditions which ultimately led to her being contracted by *The Weekly Journal*, a Swedish newspaper, to cover a story as a war correspondent on the Abyssinia Crisis. In 1935, she and Bror traveled to Ethiopia, even riding roughly 2000km by mule, to document events there.

Very much in love, Eva and Bror then traveled to New York City, where they got married in 1936. Their honeymoon was quite extravagant, a sailing trip around the Caribbean with friends, Martha Gellhorn and Ernest Hemmingway.

But Eva was not only good at controlling cars on land, but she could also fly airplanes as well, and she earned her pilot's license in 1932. And so, she set off on a number of flying expeditions, her first being from New York to Goteborg, sharing a Bellanca single-engine monoplane with Swedish pilot, Kurt Bjorkvall. Shortly after that, she returned to the US, where she boarded the

Zeppelin Hindenburg at Frankfurt, only to land five days later in Lakehurst, New Jersey.

But it had always been Eva's dream to be the first person to single-handedly cross the entire length of the Silk Road in Beijing by car. And so, on June 3rd, 1937, Eva left on her expedition and eventually crossed Germany, Poland, Romania, Turkey, Syria, and Iran.

By the time she reached Afghanistan, she was told by authorities to reconsider her route and rather travel through India, because the road through the Afghan mountains was considered too treacherous for a woman traveling alone.

She heeded the warning and changed course. On arriving in Calcutta, however, she fell very ill. She was treated with arsenic at a local hospital, but this only worsened her condition. Besides the deterioration in health, Eva also began to run out of money. By this time, the Sino-Chinese war had started, and Eva knew she would not be able to make it to her destination as planned. She had little choice but to abandon her goal and return to Europe, still feeling unwell.

She traveled for miles across desert and mountain passes, making it as far as Bagdad. This unexpected part of her journey took nine months. Needless to say, she was tired by the end, and so she chose to stopover for a few days.

Sadly, after enjoying a meal with a British friend, Norah Byng Hall of Calcutta, at a restaurant on the outskirts of Bagdad, Iraq, on driving home, she somehow lost control of her vehicle. It plummeted over the edge of a precipice, only to break her neck. She died instantly in the accident, although her friend survived.

Eva never managed to fulfil her dream of crossing the Silk Road by car, but she did everything within her power to try. With looming wars, hostilities, and other environmental factors in place, it was something she was unable to do, and it's likely that not even a man could have done so. Had the conditions been less hostile, it's almost certain she would have achieved her dream.

And so, Eva's life came to a quick end on March 24th, 1938. This brave Swedish woman, who proved most men wrong in doubting the skills of women in the field of driving, exploration, flying, and lone-survival, was only thirty-three-years-old at the time of her fatal accident.

Being so young her death was a tragedy, as she may well have gone on to achieve much more as she grew older. However, her legacy still lives on today, and she will forever be remembered as the first female Swedish rally driver and the third female Swedish aviator.

Eva Dickson was buried in Stockholm on April 22nd, 1938.

What Urged Eva to Choose the Path of Adventure?

Growing-up around horses and riding on horseback from an early age was certainly an aspect that urged Eva to be as adventurous as she was. Never having to worry financially and being allowed to express herself naturally will have helped to build her confidence. Growing up with an older brother also would have allowed her to feel safe and confident, considering they had the same friends, interests, and hobbies as well.

She was known for being mischievous but not rebellious. Rather, she reveled in her freedom. She would bring laughter to a room with her ideas and comments on different matters. With her father and mother being horse-breeders and likely keen riders, they would doubtless have been happy to see their daughter growing up strong and somewhat fearless, with a mind of her own and dreams to pursue.

She did not rely on her family for money, though, and felt it was important to be self-sufficient, which is something all strong women tend to believe. Instead of asking for money, her inventive personality prompted her to find alternatives for paying her way, like making the bet about driving across the Sahara. This was something she did often, using the money earned from winning bets to cover the expenses of her travels.

She might also have been raised in an environment where she was quite often exposed to political talk. That may have contributed to her developing a questioning mind, in order to better understand what was really going on in the world.

Perhaps she wanted to bring attention to countries that were experiencing conflict, and maybe she wanted to help out by writing about the beauty she experienced in those areas, bringing new light to them and the environment that exists beyond war. She was not only brave behind the wheel or in the cockpit of a plane, it seems that she also wanted the world to be a happier place. Perhaps she felt the best way she could help to achieve this was to document her journeys and bring a different kind of attention, other than that based on conflict, to the areas she journeyed through.

Feeling safe and secure as a child would have given her the kind of strength she needed to attempt her dreams alone.

She was talkative and extroverted, loving conversations with new people from different cultures, learning 'their side of the story' wherever she went. She was a fighter, too, and did not succumb to illness; rather, she would try to heal as quickly as possible and continue on with her plans, not allowing adversity to hold her back.

Indeed, waking up each day to a new adventure and enjoying the suspense can be an enthralling way to live for adventurers, unlike many who wake up only to go to the office to earn their living each day.

Yes, Eva was fortunate and had been dealt a good hand at the start of her life. However, the further she journeyed into perilous territories, where danger might lie in wait for her around the next corner, she was empowered to continue by the self-confidence she had built within.

Her love for adventure was likely born from her love for the outdoors and the sense of always keeping moving, which could be described more simply as wanderlust! Perhaps it was never her desire to want to be the first at something, the first woman to drive across the Sahara, for example. The titles she earned were simply by-products of her bravery and passion for new experiences. If so, then fame would not have been her main aim as much as living a life of adventure.

How Would Eva Have Prepared for Her Adventures?

As with all other adventurers, Eva would have needed to remain healthy and fit, in order to successfully complete the journeys she undertook. Being a writer as well, she would have used her education to create pieces that would leave readers spellbound, or at least open to alternative ideas about traveling to 'not-so-popular' destinations.

On preparing for a journey, she would have needed to know what such a journey would entail. An understanding of basic car mechanics would have been necessary, for times when she had to change a tire or if there was an engine failure. She would have needed to always be prepared for such things, as well as making sure she got enough rest to be able to focus on the road ahead for long hours.

She would have had to have good skills at dealing with people so she could negotiate successfully with others when necessary. The ability to think logically would have been helpful too when dealing with different situations. Some knowledge about keeping healthy and how to recognize and treat certain common illnesses in some might call 'unsafe' areas would have been vital too, as when she contracted malaria.

Because her 'sport' did not entail too much physical expenditure, she might not have needed to prepare her body each day as much her spirit. Of course, when one is embarking on a challenge that requires specific strength and skill, like tight-rope walking, one needs to both prepare body and mind for accidents, and even possible death. But driving a car cross-country would not have required that same kind of focus and finely tuned skill.

She would also have had to know how to read maps well. In those days, there was no GPS, of course. Maps were not always entirely accurate either, so she may even have created a few of her own of the areas she traveled through, which she shared through her journaled writings. In this way, she contributed her direct experience of largely uncharted, sometimes hostile territories, for those who followed her.

After all, if a young woman under the age of thirty could make it through a difficult region, then she must have found the safest way to do so. Her findings may have helped to create future maps showing easier, safer routes than previous ones. For this, she would have needed to know well how to read a compass too. Knowing how to work with the environment, especially changing weather conditions, would have been necessary as well. There were doubtless times when the roads were dangerous, and she would have had to use her intuition to determine whether or not to struggle on through or turn back and find another route.

And so, besides having a true spirit of adventure which saw her achieving tasks others would have feared to begin with, she would also have needed to be strong in her self-belief. There were certainly many times when she was alone and felt threatened, either by the natural environment, or even by thieves and gangs wanting to strip her of what she carried with her.

What Legacy Has Eva Left Behind?

A wonderful way in which Eva is remembered is through a short phrase that states, *"As a soldier dies at the battlefield, or a captain of a ship dies at sea, Eva Dickson died on the journey."*[16]

Eva was an explorer first and foremost, but also a war correspondent and travel writer whose works were valued and cherished, not just for their entertainment factor but also for their historic and cultural perspective.

Today, Eva Dickson is still spoken of for her daring journeys that saw her claim world fame as the first Swedish female rally driver as well as the third-ever female Swedish aviator. Swedish newspapers spoke greatly of her achievements, always referring to her as an adventurer when they covered her travels. Even now, authors refer to stories about her travels, and she has been featured in numerous popular books.

When someone speaks of her, they usually refer to certain aspects of her achievements, such as traveling the world, what it's like to be in the middle of a war zone, writing books and documenting events, piloting planes, crazy car races, as well as her amazing love story with a wealthy aristocrat.

Eva published numerous books about her travels as well as a number of guides, which may have helped to write more recent maps of specific territories.

She also allowed herself to be painted and drawn by some of the world's most well-known artists including Nils Dardel, Astri Taube, and Henry Goodwin. She and her husband Bror also gained attention and fame for other out-of-the-ordinary acts such as driving through Stockholm in a sports car wearing only their swimwear.

Eva was the third Swedish woman to ever obtain a pilot's license as well, which ultimately led to her being spoken about in circles of aviation too.

In Ethiopia Eva wrote about the Abyssinian crisis, as a war correspondent for the Swedish newspaper *The Weekly Journal*. One of her great stories describes her journey on the back of a mule that covered 2000km of dry and treacherous turf. She was also a war correspondent for the *Vecko-Journalen* newspaper of Abyssina, today known as Ethiopia.

In her book, *En Eva I Sahara,* she used easy to understand 'rap-like' prose, and also illustrated necessary images and shared photos she had taken on route. The book was dedicated to her love Bror and was released by Albert Bonniers Publishing House in 1933. It received rave reviews and is still available today.

She will always be remembered for her cunning and clever yet witty personality as well. One good example of this was her choosing to use the name Anton Johansson in order to enter some races that were open to men only. How does one maintain such a disguise, one must wonder?

To be the first person to drive the Silk Road had always been her dream, from the moment she discovered her love for travelling by car. She drove without a companion or 'co-pilot' through Germany, Poland, Romania, Turkey, Syria, and Iran. Although she did not complete the journey in full due to her death, she will always be remembered for this daring attempt as well.

In 2000, Lena Wisaeus created a biography of Eva's life titled, 'Eva Dickson—an Adorable Child of her Time: an Adventurous Life Journey in Words and Pictures.'

Overall, Eva had a deep love for Africa and desert terrain. When asked why she loved Africa so much, she stated, *"I believe that whoever has once been caught by the spell of Africa will never be a free person again. There you come into intimate contact with nature, enchanted and untouched by human hands, and for my part, I think that is where Africa's greatest charm lies."*[17]

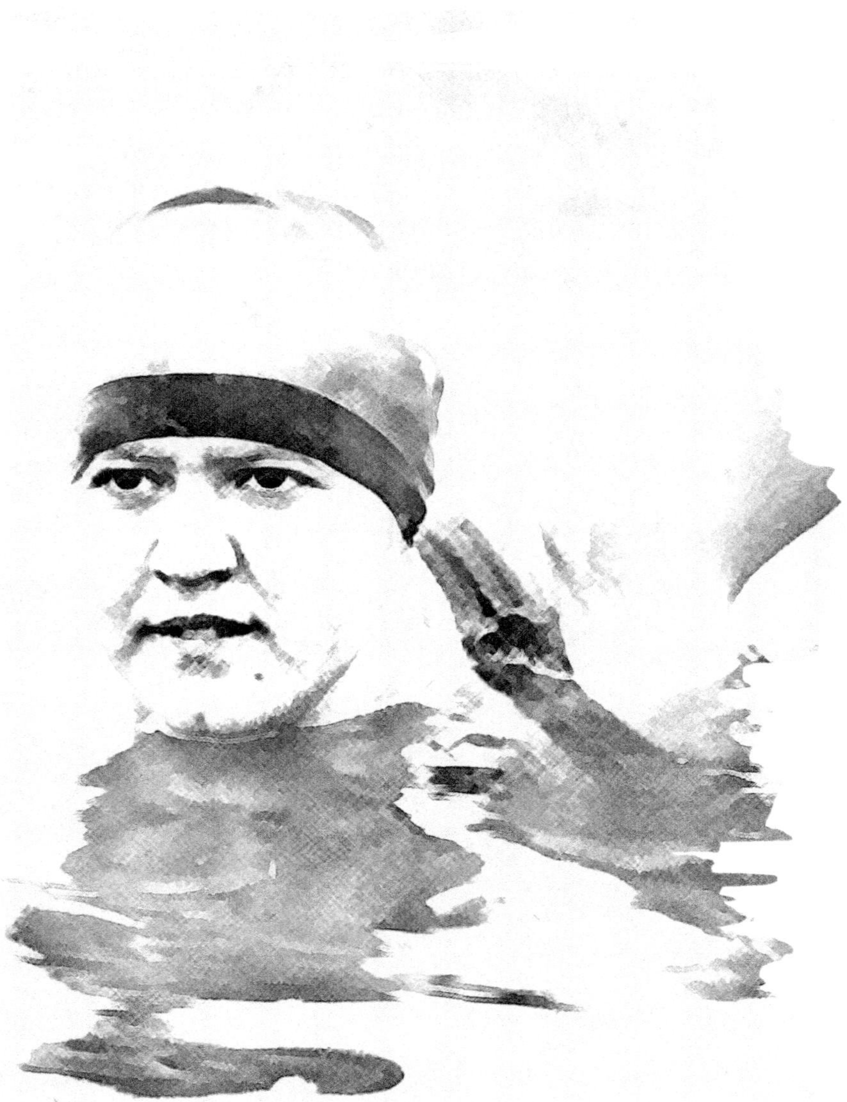

Gertrude Ederle

1905 - 2003

"To me, the sea is like a person—like a child that I've known a long time."
~ Gertrude Ederle

Who was Gertrude?

Gertrude Ederle was born in Manhattan, New York City, on October 23rd, 1906. Her father managed a butcher shop on Amsterdam Avenue in Manhattan, and was Gertrude's swimming coach. They would train at the public pool in the Highlands, New Jersey, and also in the Atlantic Ocean, where the family had a summer cottage, where they would stay during the holidays. Gertrude was the third of six children. It was clear from a young age that Gertrude was growing to be an avid and highly talented swimmer.

As a child, Gertrude contracted measles. Even though she survived, she met with complications which affected her hearing, suffering hearing-loss to almost complete deafness due to the severity of the disease. This did not change who she was, however, and she continued on with her life without allowing the disability to hold her back.

In her teenage years Gertrude left school to focus solely on swimming, as it was clear she had a natural talent for the sport. At the time, the women's bathing suit had become popular, and many women were learning to swim. Prior to this, there were rules about how women should dress when swimming. At first, their bathing outfits were bulky and cumbersome, not easy to swim in at all. But with swimming becoming popular, the Women's Swimming Association advocated for women's rights to wear comfortable and effective swimwear. The case became a mainstream issue, and it was not too long before the new and improved 'bathing suit' was introduced, which allowed women to swim more freely. However, it remained a rule that on stepping out of the pool, they would have to immediately cover themselves with a towel. Nevertheless, women's swimming slowly became competitive as a sport that had previously been for 'men-only.'

Gertrude joined the Women's Swimming Association, where she received additional training and focused on the 'crawl' stroke. She won her first local competition when she was sixteen. Passionate about swimming and dedicated to her training, she went on to set twenty-nine national and world records, with nine of these being set in a single day at a competition in New York. In 1922, she broke seven records in just one afternoon, in New York, at Brighton Beach.

Just two years after her first win, she would go on to swim in the Olympics. On arriving at the Paris Games in 1924, she had set herself the goal of winning three Olympic medals. However, at this event she won a single gold for the team event and two bronze medals for the single events she entered alone.

While she was disappointed with her results, while spending time in Paris she realized her greater purpose, her greater goal, which would be to swim the English Channel. This treacherous swim in freezing-cold waters had only been successfully done by men before. It had also been attempted by women before, but none had been successful. And so, she chose to make this her new goal: to be the first woman to successfully swim the Channel between France and England.

In 1925, she made her first attempt, stating, "*I'm not sure I'll make it, but I'll try my best.*"[18] As an American swimmer, she gained much support from American fans, and the press followed her attempts. She was somewhat patriotic about representing America, and she wanted very much to bring victory to the US.

Wearing a heavy one-piece suit that filled with water and aggravated her skin, she did not cross the full length of the Channel on this first attempt. Some criticized her, saying that the support boat had attempted to help her, thus leading to her disqualification. During long-distance swims, one of the rules was that support boats were allowed to pass food and water to swimmers, but were never allowed to physically touch them. This upset many people, who believed that this story was fabricated by the British, who did not want to see an American woman take the title.

Her trainer at the time, Bill Burgess, who had swum the channel himself, told the press she had quit because she had struggled against the tides in her cumbersome swimsuit. The strong tides meant swimmers were forced to 'zigzag' through the water, as opposed to swimming in a direct line to the other side of the Channel. This took a great physical toll. At first, Gertrude had apparently attempted to go against her trainer's decision and carry on, but having learned to trust him, she ultimately chose to agree and pull out.

This did not hinder her spirit in any way, and she would then go on to her second attempt in 1926. By this time, she was twenty years old and much stronger and better equipped to handle the tides in the Channel. For her second attempt she chose to wear a two-piece swimsuit she had designed herself, as well as motorcycle goggles to protect her eyes from the salty water. She also smothered herself in sheep-grease and lanolin, to protect her from the cold as well as jelly-fish stings.

A major incentive for Gertrude in this attempt was that her father had promised to give her a red Roadster if she crossed successfully!

On the morning of August 6th, 1926, at 07.08 in the morning, Gertrude waded into the waters with every intention of reaching her goal. *'England or Drown'* [19] was the headline that appeared in major newspapers (notably the *New York Daily News*) on that day. Indeed, Gertrude was sponsored by the *New York Daily News* as well as the *Chicago Tribune*; they covered her expenses and also provided her with a salary in return for exclusive rights to her story.

Alongside her, the support boat was filled with containers of chicken legs and jugs of vegetable and chicken soup that would give her the nourishment she needed for the swim. The boat would follow her from Cape Gris-Nez in France, all the way to Dover in England.

Besides her support boat, her media sponsors followed her on a tug as well, and the event became an all-day media broadcasting event, as they recorded her every stroke and relayed timely news back to the general public at home via wireless radios.

She began her swim and maintained her pace well until the twelfth hour of the crossing. That was when her trainer told her the winds were changing, and the water would get considerably rougher, telling here to *'get out of the water.'* Gertrude looked at her trainer and said, "What for?" Of course, having made it so far in her second attempt, she had no intention of quitting whatsoever.

After fourteen hours and thirty-one minutes in the water, Gertrude's feet made contact with the sand of the shore of Kingsdown, near Deal, in England. Looking up, she saw crowds of people waiting to greet her and celebrate not only her victory in being the first woman to cross the Channel, but also for having broken the previously set record of one hour and fifty-nine minutes—set by a man!

A journalist named Mortimer, who had followed her every stroke and was one of the first to report her accomplishment, stated, *"She's been described at the end of the swim as looking like a boxer—because the water clobbers her face. She was all bruised. And also, her tongue had swelled up so much because of the salt water, she could hardly speak. In addition, she had some jellyfish stings."*[20]

At home in America, millions greeted Gertrude at New York's very first 'ticker-tape parade' to honor a woman. President Calvin Coolidge then fondly referred to her as 'America's best girl' and invited her to the White House. Her father did indeed buy her the red Roadster he'd promised her if she succeeded!

For a few months, she was the most famous woman in the world, until other events took over the public's interest. She went on to give swimming demonstrations and even appeared in a short film about her life and career.

Sadly, she incurred a back injury in 1933, by falling down a flight of stairs, which prevented her from ever competing again. However, still being fit and limber she gave swimming performances at the Aquacade Attraction, at the New York World's Fair in 1939.

Indeed, Gertrude's success inspired other women around the world to want to attempt new challenges, especially in the sport of swimming. Gertrude held her title until 1951, when Canadian swimmer Winnie Roach-Leuszler bettered her time by an hour. Gertrude did not stop swimming; in fact, she went on to train many others in the sport, teaching swimming the Lexington School for the Deaf.

Remembered as 'Queen of the Waves,' Gertrude Ederle passed at the age if ninety-eight in Wyckoff, New Jersey, on November 30th, 2003. Her legacy lives on today in the Gertrude Ederle Recreation Center, located in the Upper West Side of Manhattan, near to where she grew-up and first learned to swim.

What Urged Gertrude to Choose the Path of Adventure?

Having been raised mostly in the water, Gertrude developed a love for swimming at a very early age. It's likely her father played an important role in her success. When a child becomes ill, most parents naturally aim to bring them back to health; Gertrude's father was no different, clearly understanding that his daughter would benefit from swimming, an excellent sport that works the entire body, as well as the mind.

After having won her first swimming event, she would have felt motivated and determined to continue competing. But with her kind of determination, she soon got to a point where she was no longer content with small wins. Instead, she chose to embark upon an adventure that would push her to her furthest limits, testing her abilities in a way that would eventually see her winning Olympic medals and gaining a world title.

Often, sporting or adventure-seeking people choose activities that push them as far as they can go, and they do this as a way to gauge the level of their own performance. They feel that if they accept the hardest of challenges and succeed, it must mean they have something above and beyond others, in terms of bravery, strength, skill, and tenacity.

Beyond the swim itself, she also had a deep desire to want to make a difference in the world for women, as with all of the other women discussed in previous chapters. It's important to keep in mind that the women represented in this book paved the way for women's inclusion in various events that were previously considered 'men only' turf.

With her disability, she carried an extra burden. Being partially deaf must have added further challenges, as being in the open waters and not being able to hear anything would have left her relying mostly on her sight. She would not have been able to hear danger approaching unless someone called out to her very loudly. She would have relied on her instincts and intuition to navigate the waters, while still attempting to remain alert to danger.

With her success at the Olympics and completing the Channel swim, she gained much fame and went on to use it to better the lives of other deaf swimmers, which can be seen through her giving demonstrations. She had learned to be headstrong and confident, and these aspects are often lacking in youngsters with disabilities. She showed to them that the human body is capable of so much more than we might at first believe, and that with the right mindset, focus, concentration, and a drive to want to succeed, folks with disabilities are capable of great things.

From a personal perspective, perhaps from a young age Gertrude found sanctuary in the waters; it would have been a quiet place away from the maddening crowds, where she could feel the water on her skin and experience the wonderful sense of freedom that buoyancy offers. She may have felt empowered at using her own strength to keep her moving forward and keep her warm too. Perhaps being submerged in the waters of the ocean offered her a sense of liberation that hearing folks could not understand. Being mostly deaf, her world would have been a quiet one. Maybe, being out in the waters, with no one around, she was able to embrace that quietude and forget about having to pretend she could understand others when they were speaking.

The ocean would have been her place of solace, as it has often been said that the waters of the ocean hold great secrets for those who listen from the heart, which is what Gertrude did.

With the help of her supportive family, and a desire to want to spend time in silence, hearing the ocean speak to her through its currents, temperatures, and sea life, she became world famous for her tenacity and endurance. While she only reached success on her second attempt when crossing the English Channel, even when she was advised to get out of the water, she knew she had already achieved far too much to jeopardize her win. It was a 'make or break' moment for her, a time when she decided to push through despite the jellyfish stings, cramps, and cold.

For Gertrude, these harsh external elements may well have matched her internal world; not being able to hear others must have been frustrating for her. Yet with swimming, she learned to keep going and listen to her inner voice so as to achieve whatever she set out to.

How Would Gertrude Have Prepared for Her Adventures?

Because swimming is a sport that requires peak fitness, Gertrude would have needed to concentrate a great deal on staying fit, as well as expanding her ability to withstand the cold temperatures of the water.

It is a known fact that training the body to tolerate environmental impacts or changes through submerging it in cold water serves to strengthen both it and the mind. When the body is tolerant of external forces, the mind becomes stronger, so less energy is spent on worrying about physical pains and niggles and more on focusing on and achieving goals.

Gertrude would have needed to eat well too, for the best defense against illness or adverse ailments is a healthy diet. She would have eaten a lot of carbs to keep her energy levels up, and also would have consumed much magnesium to keep her muscular system functioning at optimum levels.

She would also have needed to be able to tolerate insult and judgement because, at the time, women were not supposed to partake in swimming, since doing so meant they would have to reveal too much naked skin, which was seen as socially unacceptable. Unlike men, they did not even have their own comfortable bathing suits to swim in! Men would have perhaps teased her or even mocked her for trying to compete in a man's world. And so, Gertrude would have had to develop strong self-esteem and confidence as well, not letting mean comments or insults from others upset her. If she had done so, she would doubtless have felt insecure and given up swimming altogether.

In funding her swims and achievements, Gertrude did not have the flirtatious, outgoing personality that many bold women of the time seem to have possessed. It is true that many women who achieved great things were able to fund their way due to their looks or engaging personalities. Men favored brave and pretty women to invest in, finding them 'entertaining' and worth the money spent. But those who invested in Gertrude did so because of her talent and drive to want to achieve something which had not been achieved before. In order to gain their sponsorship, she had to prove herself in the water, as opposed to merely modeling for them in her swimsuit!

Gertrude would also have encouraged others who wanted to attempt great things, especially among the deaf community. She would have used her highly developed empathy and compassion for others to secure engagement through conversation and action.

Although she was tough, her empathy was obvious in the way she freely offered her time and skills to train other deaf swimmers, to help them to reach for their dreams too.

Above all, Gertrude would have needed to be trusting of others. With her hearing disability, she knew she could not rely on hearing their calls or commands when it was necessary. Instead, she would have had to trust others' touch and the signs they made to communicate with her, so she would have had to be comfortable with making good eye-contact.

For some with disabilities, making eye-contact can be a challenge, but for Gertrude it would have been one of the only ways to determine the conditions in her immediate environment. She had to be able to understand facial expressions and body language, to ensure she received the right information about what was going on around her during her long swims. The ability to fully trust those who worked with her was vital to her wellbeing, as she relied completely on them to alert her when her life was in danger, whether through physical reaction to the cold waters, or through running out of energy and at risk of drowning.

Overall, it is certain that Gertrude developed a strong mind-over-matter outlook on life, using her determination and skills to persevere through harsh conditions when the body may have chosen to give up. Her mind-body connection would have been strong, and in order to maintain this strength, she had to be in total control of her body and senses at all times.

What Legacy Has Gertrude Left Behind?

Perhaps Gertrude grew up with the dream of being a famous world champion swimmer, even if such a title was not available to women at the time. Her perseverance led her to achieve what she did, and the timing was just right as well, for she was at her fittest when the moment came for women to participate in major sporting events for the first time in history.

Besides being remembered as bold, courageous, tenacious, and somewhat patriotic, she began her career through securing a number of titles in the sport of swimming.

Some of the titles she secured, beyond 'Queen of the Waves,' include:

- Olympic Champion

- World record holder in five events

- The first woman to swim the English Channel

On her return to Manhattan after swimming the English Channel, it is said that more than two million people lined the streets of the parade to cheer for her.

Edward L. Hyman, a well-known theater manager and innovator, arranged for her to make an appearance at the Brooklyn Mark Strand, where she received higher pay for her performance than any individual performer had ever before been offered.

She appeared in a movie about her life, titled *Swim Girl, Swim*. She also met President Coolidge, a great honor, and even had a dance step named after her!

Gertrude was introduced to the International Swimming Hall of Fame as an Honor Swimmer in 1965, and then into the National Women's Hall of Fame in 2003.

In New York City, an annual swim from New York City's Battery Park to Sandy Hook in New Jersey is named after Gertrude: The

Ederle Swim. The course follows the same route she took during one of her very first competitive swims.

In Manhattan we find the Gertrude Ederle Recreation Center, also named after her.

Then, in 2010 and 2012, BBC 4 broadcast a play titled *The Greta Swim*, based on a book by Gavin Mortimer, written in 2008. It covered Gertrude's dramatic Channel crossing.

At the time of writing this book, Walt Disney Pictures has acquired the rights to a screenplay based on the book by Glenn Stout titled *Young Woman of the Sea*. The movie will be directed by Joachim Ronning, with Daisy Ridley playing the role of Gertrude.

Without a doubt, she left a mark on many women, especially women swimmers, and she will always be remembered for her accomplishments and bravery.

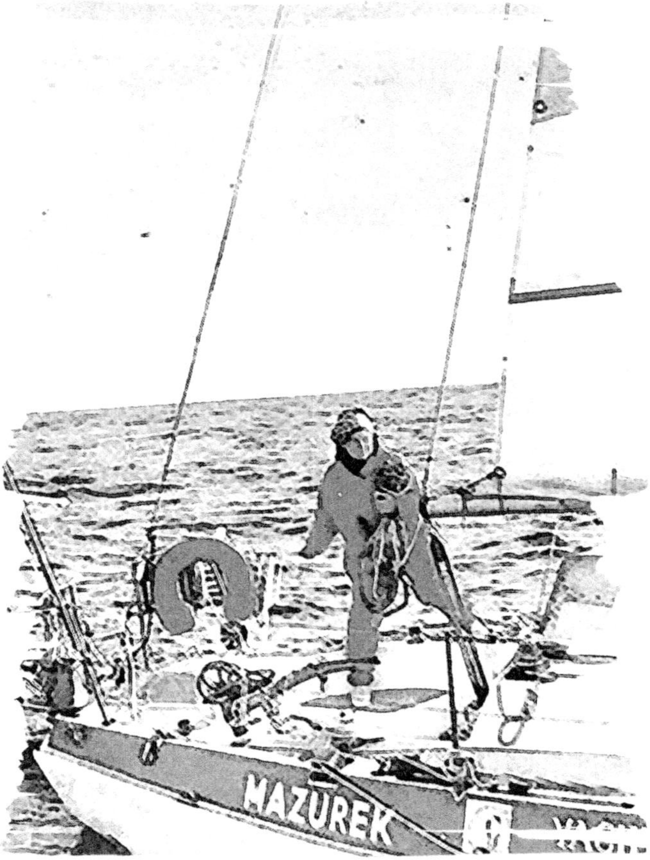
MAZUREK

Krystyna Chojnowska

1936 - 2021

> *"I'm not afraid of what I don't know, although normal people are said to have it the other way around."*
> ~ Krystyna Chojnowska

Who was Krystyna?

Krystyna Chojnowska-Liskiewicz was born in Warsaw, Poland, on July 15th, 1936.

After the Second World War, her family moved away from the capitol and headed for the Great Lakes, namely the Great Masurian Lakes in northeastern Poland. There, they hoped to find a more peaceful life, as their previous home had become part of the city's overcrowded Jewish ghetto.

They settled in a small town called Ostroda, right next to the lakes. There, Krystyna was amazed by the number of boats on the waters and was especially intrigued by the larger ships. This led her to want to study boats and boating, and so she enrolled at the Shipbuilding Department of the Gdansk University of Technology, where she studied ship construction engineering. This was an unusual choice for women at the time as boating, building boats, and engineering had always been considered subjects for men only.

During this time she fell in love with Waclaw Liskiewicz, a classmate of hers at the university. He would go on to work as a constructor at the yacht shipyard in Gdansk. Once Krystyna graduated with an engineering degree, she also found work at the Gdansk Shipyard, working in both design and construction. She soon obtained a design patent for a yacht helmsman's chair, and shortly after that for a sea helmsman's chair. In 1966, she was given her license for yachting, earning her the title "Captain of Great Sailing."

Krystyna set sail with a crew on a few occasions before deciding to sail around the world on her own. This experience of working with a crew gave her the hands-on experience she would need as a lone sailor, and also allowed her to better understand the deeper waters and what to do in dire situations. Her first trip with an all-women crew was from Szczecin to Warnemunde (then East Germany). With that success under their belts, they sailed from Poland to Scotland, where they were met by local fishermen who were astonished that there was not a single man on board. After that, she sailed with a colleague from the Gulf of Bothnia to the Northern Baltic Sea.

Around that time, the United Nations had begun its campaign to improve the lives of women, allowing them the opportunity to do things they'd not previously been permitted to do. This involved promoting their inclusion into the various forms of competitive sports, business, invention, innovation, and pioneering.

The Polish Sailing Association saw this as the perfect opportunity to promote women's sailing. It aimed to send the first solo female sailor around the world on a yacht. Not only would it be a world's first for women, but also for Poland. When the applicants were considered, Krystyna's name was on the list, and it was not too difficult for the Association members to choose her above the rest, due to her training, experience, and sheer love for boating and the open waters.

And so, not only was Krystyna selected to become the first woman to sail around the world, her husband was also given the task of building her yacht. He custom-built the boat for her, which they then named *Mazurek*, after a genre of traditional Polish music. The boat was equipped with all the provisions Krystyna would need, as well as the relevant tools, maps, necessary reading materials, and a shotgun for protection. The *Mazurek* was a 'Conrad 32 sloop', 9.51m (31.2ft) in length, with a beam of 2.70m (8.86ft), and a sail area of 35m^2 (376.7 ft^2).

It was decided that she would begin her journey from the Canary Islands, covering a distance of 28,500 miles when crossing the Atlantic, sailing through the Panama Canal, and then crossing the Pacific to Australia. The yacht built by Waclaw was transported to the Islands, and her date of departure was set for March 10th, 1976.

On March 10th, she headed out to deeper waters and was cheered on by hundreds of sailors and boat-lovers, who wanted very much to see her complete the round-the-world trip safely and successfully.

All looked good until, around one month into her journey, the autohelm malfunctioned, and she was left with no choice but to head to shore for repairs. She'd reached her first destination, Barbados, and then Panama mostly by sail as the engine was malfunctioning. With the repairs completed, which took around five weeks, she then headed back out into the waters. Despite having lost almost three weeks on her schedule, she had no intention of giving up and hoped she'd make up the lost time further on along her journey when the winds were in her favor.

After navigating through the Panama Canal, she headed to the Marquesas Islands via the Pacific Ocean, a journey that took almost two months. To avoid boredom and to keep the ship maintained, she would dedicate each day of the week to different sections of the boat. She would also discuss various technical and maritime issues with her husband over radiotelephone every couple of days.

On arriving in Tahiti, she was overwhelmed by the beauty of the place. She then moved on to Fiji and Australia. It was there, in Sydney, after being apart for just over a year, that she met up with her husband again. They explored the nearby cities together, while the boat went in for minor repairs and renewal of worn parts. It was here that she was interviewed by various presenters from well-known TV shows, which saw her popularity grow across the globe.

Then, in May, she headed toward the Great Barrier Reef, navigating her way through it during the days, while anchoring at night. In July she arrived at Portland Road, Australia, where she was met by doctors, who transported her to the hospital, as she had been feeling unwell. It was soon discovered she was suffering with kidney stones. While she was being treated and nurtured back to health, her boat broke its anchor line and drifted out to sea. It was feared missing for a few days, but fortunately, it was soon spotted and returned without any damage being caused.

Once she was feeling well again, she set out to Darwin to prepare for the next leg of her journey, which would see her sail across the Indian Ocean to Mauritius, and then on to South Africa. Along this part of the journey, she again had complications with the autohelm, and she was forced to steer the yacht manually for the rest of the way, only allowing herself two hours of sleep per day.

She soon arrived in Cape Town, and, while resting there for a few days, heard that another woman was also attempting a trip around the world by boat, namely New Zealand's Naomi

James. Not to be pipped at the post, Krystyna left Cape Town on February 3rd, crossing the Atlantic Ocean for seventy-five days before finally reaching Barbados on March 20th, 1978.

This was a difficult section for her to sail through. Some fierce storms left folks wondering if she'd become lost or drowned, as they could not connect with her via radio. It was only in early March that the Polish Antarctic Station was able to make contact. The world was relieved to hear from her, and she explained that the final leg of her journey had been 'like a stroll' compared to what she'd been through already. Once she'd completed her journey of 28,696 nautical miles, she told the Polish Press Agency, "*I think I can do without sailing for some time now!*"

After a few months of excitement, recognition, and interviews, as well as attending various award ceremonies, where she was granted titles such as *The Most Outstanding Polish Sailor of All Time*, and the *First Woman in the World to Circumnavigate the Earth Alone on a Sailing Yacht*, she decided to settle down, working at the Radunia Shipyard until her retirement in Gdansk.

Krystyna passed on June 12th, 2021, at the age of eighty-four, and she will always be remembered as being the first woman to sail solo around the world by yacht. She will also be honored for changing the scope of sailing, by being one of the first women to not only compete in sailing challenges, but also to complete a task that had initially only been seen as accomplishable by men.

On the topic of women in adventurous and challenging sports, she stated, "*With malicious joy, I thought about the many captains who compulsorily herd women in mixed crews into pots. They often lose good steersmen, navigators, mechanics, sailmakers, officers, and they have a chance of indigestion. And I know some excellent cooks-sailors—*"[21], implying that it is waste for men to choose women crew members as cooks and chefs only when it is clear they are capable of so much more.

What Urged Krystyna to Choose the Path of Adventure?

Having grown-up on the Great Masurian Lakes, Krystyna gained great satisfaction and peace out on the waters while boating. Her family had fled from the city, where life was becoming too busy and distracting in the wake of rebuilding after the war. Her family clearly felt that finding a home in more natural surroundings was both safer than in the city and more motivating.

As a child she wanted to know all there was to know about boats and sailing, and this can be seen through her choice to attend the University of Technology, in the Shipbuilding Department of the Gdansk University, where she studied ship-construction engineering. It was not so much that she wanted to learn more about how to sail, rather she wanted to know how ships were built, so she could contribute her 'engineering mind' to the world of boating. And, of course, she dreamed of one day taking to the seas in her own boat—without needing the assistance of a man.

During her earlier years, and at the onset of her first entry into competitive sailing, she was criticized, as most women were then, for attempting to enter a sphere dominated by men. She was small and brave, and she did not bother herself too much with the opinions of others. Instead, she knew what she wanted to do and went ahead, remaining focused on her own wellbeing and skills, as opposed to being swayed by those who did not believe in her.

When Poland was facing the terrible aftermath of war, young people there seldom wanted anything to do with city life and the troubles it presented. Being on the waters allowed Krystyna complete peace of mind, where all she needed to do was survive in her own capacity. It was a test of survival for her, mixed with a need to be away from the trials of everyday life. Beyond that, at a professional level, she believed women were equally as skilled as men and wanted very much to show them that she was capable of performing the same tasks.

Her opportunity arose when the Polish Sailing Association chose to actively partake in the 'Year of the Woman,' and initiative launched by the United Nations in 1975. In doing so, the Polish People's Republic would become internationally recognized. She had competition, though, for at the time, Austrian sailor Waltraud Meyer was also aiming to become the first woman to sail around the world by boat.

And so, we can see that the stage was set for her embarking on her journey not only by the need to bring attention to Poland, but also the wish for the region to achieve something great—in this case, as home to the first woman who sailed around the world alone by yacht. Krystyna was obviously enthralled at being given the task, which must have been a dream come true for a young girl who grew up on the Lakes.

But back in those days there was no Google Earth and no GPS. If someone wanted to see the world, they could not rely solely on images and information sent back from other explorers. They had to go out on their own to find the magical wonders of the world, even if it meant them placing their life in danger.

Krystyna was filled with wanderlust, and her method of movement or transport was a yacht. Out there on the ocean, she likely felt she was living a life worth living, in the sense that she would be using all of her human elements and strengths to survive a dimension of existence that very few ever get to experience. The currents and waves and swells in the ocean were equally, if not more, daunting than the threat of bombs or weaponry. Perhaps she felt that if she was going to live a life under some form of threat, it would be best to face natural threats amid nature's magnificence than any posed by humanity.

There must have been many hours, days, and even weeks when she would not see land or make any contact with other people whatsoever. During these times, she would have doubtless contemplated many things in life, thus helping her to form a philosopher's mind that would inevitably help her to better understand the nature of life itself.

A strong sense of self-sufficiency would have been one of her major motivations, especially after her family had been forced to leave her place of birth, due to their area being made part of Warsaw's Jewish ghetto, the largest in the world. Through this, she would have seen desperation in others and the fights that arise from inequality or lack of various resources. Being self-sufficient meant she would never need to rely on others to survive.

Even when she fell ill she did not let it stop her from making progress. One can only imagine how it must feel to be ill on a boat in the middle of the ocean with no one around to help you. That, indeed, would build great strength and self-reliance.

But she would go beyond just the simple need to survive—she would go on to thrive as well, and show others, through her writings, that there is far more to life than simply sitting around 'waiting for your ship to come in'!

How Would Krystyna Have Prepared for Her Adventures?

Krystyna had the advantage of being raised to enjoy the waters on a boat. Fear of depths and drowning were not barriers to her, and she had complete confidence in her ability to manage the waters in various conditions. However, if she was to go on to sail the world alone, she needed to know every name of every part of a boat, and how each of those parts work, individually and together. While she may have been able to call a coastguard when in range, there were also times when she would have had to wait for days for help to arrive, and so she had to be fully prepared for all possible complications.

She would also have needed to be prepared mentally. It is one thing to live in a dream of adventuring around the world, but quite another to find oneself in the middle of the ocean with no one around. Some people may well have suffered from being deprived of social interaction on such a voyage. Some may have become frightened at the conditions on the water, or even found themselves going mad under the relentless sun! But Krystyna was well prepared mentally and, of course, always had a pen and paper with her, to record her experiences and feelings, thus preventing the potentially overwhelming feeling of being alone.

She would have needed to be fit and healthy as well and had a good knowledge of which foods to take with her so as to maintain her health. After all, there is only so much space on a yacht, and there certainly were no stores nearby to purchase any groceries! Therefore, she must have had to sacrifice many enjoyable things, even simple things like a roast dinner on Sunday or a glass of wine. Simplicity and minimalism would have been key to her survival.

Most of all, she would have needed to know how to handle danger by keeping a sound mind and taking a rational approach to challenges. Without the ability to remain calm in tough conditions as well as her skills and knowhow, she may have been forced to return home from her journey without accomplishing her goal.

Of course, she would also have needed to know how to read nautical maps, work with environmental and weather changes, and have at least a basic understanding of the various languages she would encounter along the way.

Overall, for Krystyna, one can be sure that her main motivation for setting out on her ocean adventures was a desire to experience life alone, without the influence of others, in order to reach her own conclusions about her purpose. This may well have been a superior motivator, over and above the need for any fame she would inevitably receive.

What Legacy Has Krystyna Left Behind?

Krystyna is not only remembered for being the first woman to sail solo around the world on a yacht, but she is also admired and remembered for her perseverance in encouraging and establishing the inclusion of women in a sporting endeavor that was previously seen as the realm of men.

While women had sailed before, in those days, they were usually only taken along for the ride as cooks or chefs, cooking meals for the crew. They were seldom assigned positions as captains, helmsmen, engineers, or boat constructers.

We can learn all about her journey through her book *Pierwsza Dookoła Świata* (*The First to Sail Around the World*), which she wrote in 1979. This book is still available today and is often used as guide to new-comers to the sport of sailing.

Some positions she held after her major accomplishment include:

- Being selected as a member of the jury of the 'Cruise of the Year' and 'Kolosy' Awards

- Being a member of the Sea Sailing Committee of the Polish Sailing Association

- Krystyna was awarded the Commander's Cross of the Order of Polonia Restituta

- She also received a gold medal for Outstanding Sports Achievements

- She was awarded the silver medal of the Ministry of Sport and Youth of the Republic of France

In 1978, she received one of the most prestigious awards given for sailing in Poland, namely the 'Silver Sextant.'

On the 45th anniversary of her round-the-world achievement, the Seymik (Council) of the Pomeranian Sailing Association accepted her as an honorary member by acclamation.

Indeed, her achievement was also recorded in the Guinness Book of Records. Launching in March of 1976, Krystyna journeyed around the world by yacht covering 28,696 nautical miles (or 46,000 kilometers) over a period of 401 days.

Krystyna, although no longer with us, will hold her title forever. While some may feel that being alone on a yacht in the middle of hurricane-ridden waters by choice is akin to digging an early grave, she showed the world that women certainly are as capable as men of achieving great things through adventure.

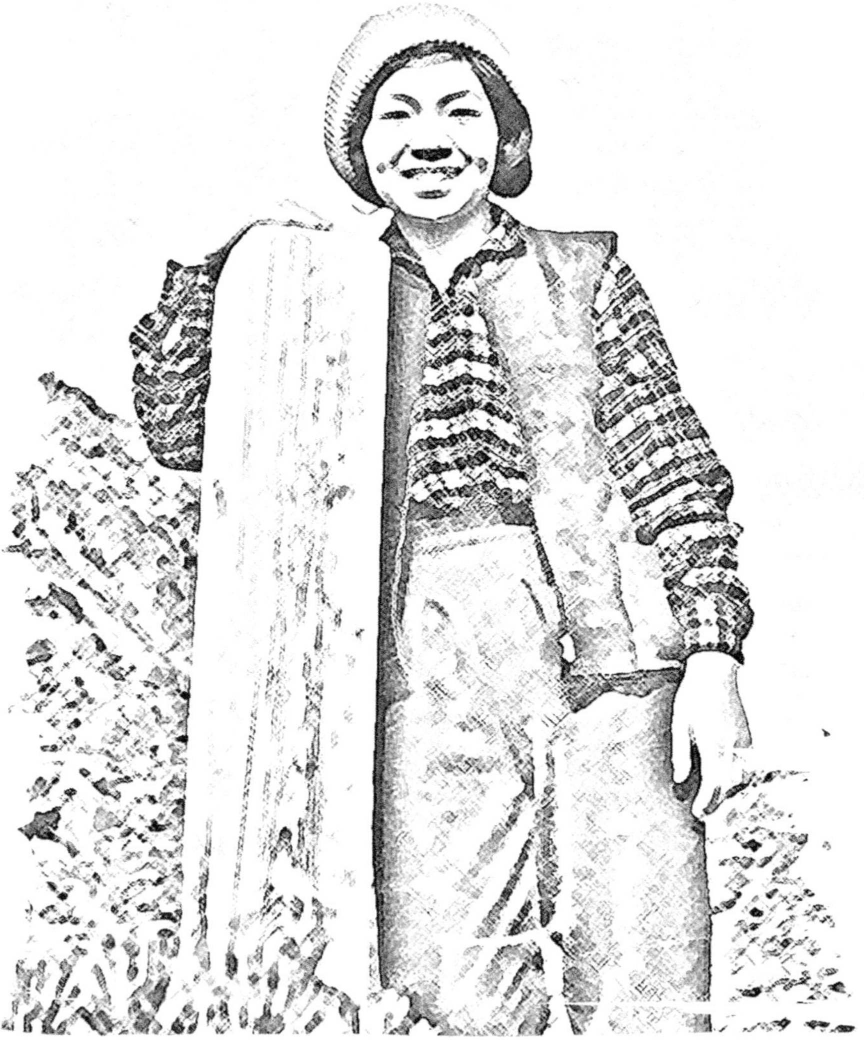

Junko Tabei

1939 - 2016

"Technique and ability alone do not get you to the top; it is the willpower that is the most important."
~ Junko Tabei

Who was Junko?

Junko Tabei was born Junko Ishibashi on September 22nd, 1939, in Miharu, near Fukushima in Japan. She was the fifth child in a family of seven children. Junko was known during her childhood as being somewhat 'frail,' in the sense that she was neither boisterous nor aggressive, with quite a passive and uncompetitive nature in times of conflict or challenge.

Besides being small and a little 'fragile,' she enjoyed the outdoors and was always captivated by the beauty of nature, choosing to follow her exploratory heart rather than remain in an office behind a desk. Her first mountain-climbing adventure was to Mount Nasu, a journey she made with her classmates at the early age of ten.

Unfortunately, when she was a child, her parents could not afford to nurture and encourage her love for climbing because of the expense involved in providing equipment, accommodation, and travel to the sites she wanted to explore.

In her younger years, Junko attended all the mountaineering trips she could within her family's budget, and she would later go on to climb some of the most famous peaks in the world throughout her climbing career, including Mount Everest.

From 1958 through to 1962, Junko attended the Showa Women's University in Tokyo, where she studied English and American literature, as she had initially wanted to pursue a career as a teacher. Once she'd received her degree, she joined a few climbing clubs that mostly consisted of men, if not entirely. While some enjoyed her being with them on their climbs, others objected to women being allowed to climb with men, saying it was a 'dangerous' sport that required muscle and endurance. Nevertheless, by her mid-twenties, she had climbed all major mountains in Japan, including Mount Fuji.

At the age of twenty-seven, Junko married a mountaineer she'd met while climbing Mount Tanigawa, Masanobu Tabei. Together, they had one son, Shinya, and one daughter, Noriko.

With a passion for climbing, and wanting other women to embark on such fantastical journeys, she established the Joshi-Tohan Club (the Women's Mountaineering Club), which was exclusive to women. She funded much of the project, as well as her own climbs, through working as an editor for Japan's *Journal of Physical Society* and teaching piano. The club itself also raised funds through making climbing equipment like gloves and sleeping bags, as well crowdfunding through the *Yomiuri Shimbun* newspaper and Nippon Television. The members still had to pay much of their own way, though, with their eventual Everest climb costing 1.5-million-yen per member. The club's slogan was 'Let's go on an overseas expedition by ourselves,' and it was the first of its kind in Japan.

The women went on their first major trip in 1970, when Junko and one team-mate ascended to the peak of the Annapurna III, a Nepalese mountain, on May 19th. The club's success gained the women titles for the first females as well as the first from Japan to tackle the climb. Only Junko and one other climber, Hiroko Hirakawa, were chosen to make the final climb to the top, accompanied by two Sherpa guides. The pair took a camera with them to record the moment, but the cold temperatures inevitably cracked the film.

With the Mount Everest climb as their major goal, they applied for a permit in 1971, calling their club the Japanese Women's Everest Expedition, which was to be led by Eiko Hisano. They waited for four years to receive their formal climbing schedule.

In May of 1975, the team was finally able to begin its expedition. Press and media agents accompanied the women for the first part of their journey, which began along the same route used by Sir Edmund Hilary and Tenzing Norgay in 1953. Six Sherpa guides joined the women and stayed with them from start to finish.

However, on May 4th, while camping at 6,300-meters, an avalanche truck their camp, leaving Junko and four other members trapped beneath the snow. Junko lost consciousness but was soon dug out by the Sherpas. There were no fatalities, but Junko had to spend two days recovering from the incident.

While it had been the plan that Junko would get to the peak of Everest with one other climber, due to the threat of altitude sickness and the Sherpas being unable to carry as many oxygen tanks as would be needed, the team leader, Eiko Hisano, nominated Junko to be the one who would make the final climb alone with the Sherpas.

Junko almost backed out very near the top, when she came to a ridge of ice that was extremely thin and slippery—a ridge that had never been spoken of during discussions back at basecamp.

After returning home, she stated in an interview with the *Japan Times* – "*I had no idea I would have to face that, even though I'd read all the accounts of previous expeditions. I got so angry at the previous climbers who hadn't warned me about that knife-edge traverse in their expedition records.*"[22]

It was a 'do or die' moment for Junko. Knowing she had given most of her life to the climb, she managed to pick her way across the ridge, and on May 16th, 1975, she became not only the first Japanese woman to reach the summit, but the first woman in the world to reach the summit. The Sherpa accompanying her was Ang Tsering. As a climber, Junko was the thirty-sixth person to reach the peak and descend successfully.

Junko was praised all around the world for her achievement, and this only spurred her to want to try new, more challenging climbs. From Everest, she went on to climb the highest mountains across all continents, including:

Mt. Kilimanjaro (in 1980)
Mt. Aconcagua (in 1987)
Mt. Denali (in 1988)
Mt. Elbrus (in 1989)
Mt. Vinson (in 1991)
Mt. Puncak Jaya (in 1992)

With Puncak Jaya under her belt, she became recognized as the first woman in history to complete the Seven Summits Challenge.

By 2005, Junko had completed forty-four mountaineering expeditions with all-female teams, and by the end of her career she had climbed seventy of the world's tallest mountains.

Beyond her climbing career, she turned to environmentalism, focusing on Mount Everest and its degraded environment; it was, and still is, littered with discarded equipment and trash left by climbers who don't care about the mountain's preservation. She also formed an association focusing on environmental protection in 2010, called the Himalayan Adventure Fund.

In 2012, Junko was unfortunately diagnosed with stomach cancer. She continued climbing even during treatment, which included a trip to Mt. Fiji with a group of youths in 2016. This would ultimately be her last major climb, as she passed later that year at a hospital in Kawagoe, Japan, on October 20th.

Junko led the way for many women around the world. She once said of women in general, *"We were told we should be raising children instead."*[23] But she achieved so much and, in turn, reshaped the future for women in sports and adventure climbing.

What Urged Junko to Choose the Path of Adventure?

Junko was the fifth-born child in a family of seven children. Even in her older years she was seen as small and even somewhat fragile, in the sense that she never exerted dominance over others, preferring rather to stick to her own goals and manifest them. That was what was most important to her—to achieve what she set out to without 'climbing' on the backs of others.

Living in a small home with so many siblings would also have contributed to her wanderlust, for although having family is great, there are times when we want to explore ourselves and discover aspects of life on our own. That explains why we often feel we need time alone in nature, simply as a way to understand life and ourselves better.

Being labeled 'fragile' might also have given her the extra spur she needed to achieve what she did. Perhaps she wanted to prove to others that it doesn't matter how small and 'fragile' you appear, it is what you are capable of that really matters. While many disagreed with her being allowed to climb mountains and compete with others in the field of mountaineering, she chose to remain respectful and quietly pursue all avenues to success she could find.

Also, being small might have been what made the mountains so appealing to her. They are vast landscapes of great beauty but threatening at the same time, and she had learned that, like a rose with its thorns, the two often go hand in hand.

Again, it was likely not her intention to prove to others that women could be climbers and mountaineers. Rather, climbing was something she really wanted to do, to see the view from the top, to accept and overcome the challenges faced by our bodies in adverse environments, and to reach new heights, of course. It is noted that she did not enjoy being famous and often felt the tributes paid to her were unnecessary. She was, indeed, humble yet highly motivated, with fame being a mere side effect of her accomplishments. In fact, after receiving much attention for being the first woman to climb Everest, she asked the media to refer to her as the '36th person' to have made the ascent.

She was always willing to work with others, though, and never found any need to want to dominate or lead a group. The choice was made for her to be the one to make it to the top of Mount Everest with the Sherpas; she did not demand to be chosen. She was selected and accepted it as an honor. She was respectful, mindful, courteous, communicative, responsive, and inspired by challenges presented by nature. She seemed to know that if she could overcome the challenges posed by such huge mountains, then dealing with life's little problems would be a breeze.

How Would Junko Have Prepared for Her Adventures?

Perhaps the mindset that spurred Junko onward was the idea that if something could be done, why should she not be the one to do it? If there was a challenge to be faced, why should she not be the one to face it, alone?

She was clearly not at all egotistical, for she disliked the fame her adventures brought her. Evidently, she enjoyed challenging herself and was far from selfish. Junko had the ability to focus on her chosen goal, putting blinkers on to prevent any negative influences from steering her away from what she believed was possible.

As with all the other women who have achieved great things through adventure, she would have needed to remain fit and healthy, not only to withstand the physical challenges she faced on her climbs, but also the altitude and air pressure changes found at great heights.

With her health and fitness secured, Junko had to find her own sponsors to fund her adventures in climbing. Her parents had no money to help her, so all of the journeys she made, she either funded herself, or she managed to find a sponsor to help her. She earned her way by making paid public appearances, guiding mountain-climbing teams, tutoring local children in music and English, and accepting donations in the form of food, equipment, and clothing.

Junko would also, somehow, have needed to be prepared for death throughout most of her climbs. This requires great concentration, an example being when she chose to cross the thick ice-ledge on Mount Everest which she saw for the first time on route. No one had prepared her for this perilous section, and the chances of falling to her death were extremely high. Meditation would have been a valuable tool for her in staying calm and being able to make good choices, as it was seldom that anyone around her could make them for her.

Junko put a lot back into the environment as well, and this must also have been one of the motivating factors that kept her going. Through her environmental projects, she aimed to keep the mountains clean from the debris and rubbish that others left behind after their climbs. Junko would become upset at seeing rubbish along the trails and spent much of her time bringing the issue to the people's attention.

For someone of her small size, Junko had more motivation than most to achieve what she set out to, and none of it was based on her own selfish need for fame or recognition. Instead, she climbed as a way to be in nature at its most formidable and face all it had to offer, perhaps to learn as much as she could about herself and life by immersing herself in nature's awesome power.

What Legacy Has Junko Left Behind?

Besides becoming the very first woman to make it to the top of Mount Everest, and the first Japanese woman to do so, Junko's life was dotted with prestigious accolades which allowed her to be more than 'just a mountaineer.'

Some of her most important achievements include:

- Junko was the first woman to ascend the Seven Summits, climbing the highest peaks across every continent.

- Junko wrote several books throughout her life, all focusing on the environment and mountaineering, including *Honoring High Places,* a book that is highly regarded among mountaineers still today.

- Junko was praised for her efforts at organizing environmental projects to clean up the mountains, clearing the trails of rubbish left behind by careless mountaineers.

- She was also praised for leading annual climbs of Mount Fuji for youths who had experienced hardship and trauma during the Great East Japan Earthquake.

- Junko had a comet named after as well, namely Asteroid 6897 Tabei.

- In 2019, a mountain range on the planet of Pluto was named Tabei Montes in her honor, with the theme being, '*Historic pioneers who crossed new horizons in the exploration of the Earth, sea and sky.*'[3]

- On making the Everest climb successfully, Junko received goodwill messages from the King of Nepal as well as the Japanese Government.

- A TV series was made about the expedition, and Junko made special personal appearances across Japan to promote it.

- In 2000, Junko completed her postgraduate studies at Kyushu University.

- She would go on to become Director of the Himalayan Adventure Trust of Japan.

- In September 2019, Google celebrated her 80th birthday through a doodle on their home page, accompanied by a slogan that said, '*Do not give up. Keep on your quest.*'

Among other acknowledgements and achievements, Junko Tabei will always be remembered for being the first woman to climb Everest—despite her request to rather be referred to as the 36th mountaineer to make the climb.

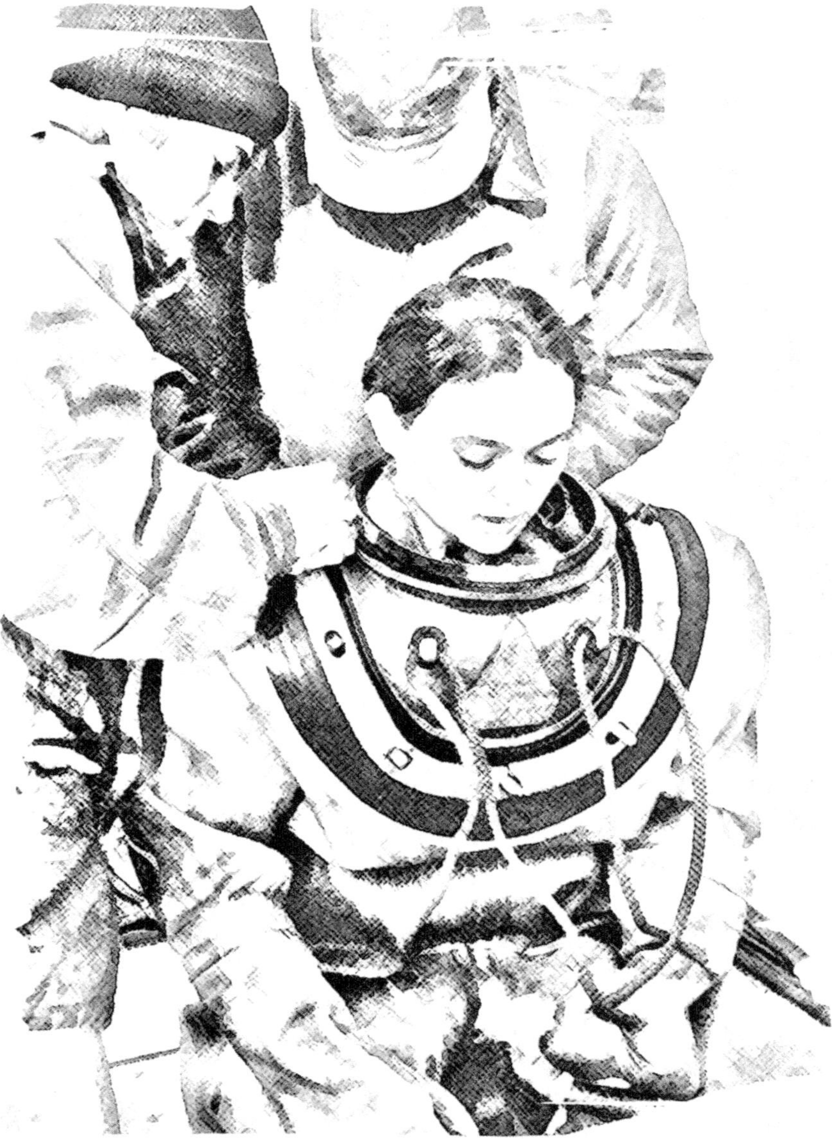

Donna Tobias

1952 - 2010

"If you ever uttered the words, 'I quit,' you could never take them back, and there were plenty of eyes waiting to see me fail."
~ Donna Tobias

Who was Donna?

Donna Tobias was born in Los Angeles, California, on May 22nd, 1952. Her father, Elmer, had been a World War II bomber crewman and, eventually, a prisoner of war. After the war, he secured work as an electromagnetics manufacturer. Her mother was a housewife and stay-at-home mom, and she had a brother too. The family did not have much money, but their parents did the best they could to make sure the children went to school and had a good childhood.

Donna's childhood was simple, yet she displayed a love for humanity that saw her helping others whenever she could. In her school there were numerous underprivileged kids with problems. Donna would connect with them and was known as being sincerely interested in their wellbeing. She always fought for equal treatment with empathy, expressing her opinions about society's failures. She was known to have intense conversations at times over topics of importance.

She loved the ocean more than anything, and after school each day, she would go out to the bay at Long Island Sound to swim and snorkel. She also followed folklore, as was seen through her placing blue glass bottles upside down on tree branches to keep evil spirits away. She collected things, too, like pretty stones and empty birds' nests, and also works of art. An old friend of hers, Judith Rosenberg, stated about her home, *"It was a maze of art, an internal labyrinth. Everywhere you turned, there was something to look at."*[25]

Donna also turned her garage into a studio, where she carved in wood and stone, while listening to African and Caribbean music.

After graduating from high school in Anaheim, she went to work as a school bus driver, and also worked in the police department, while taking free classes at Fullerton College.

Perhaps wanting to see what life had been like for her father in the navy, she then applied to join the US Navy in 1974. She had initially wanted to be a diver, but at that time, it was not a position available to women. So, she joined the ship-fitting and hull technical team, while applying for dive-school, which required her to have a letter of permission from the Pentagon.

In 1973, Kati Garner became the first female US Navy diver, and this paved the way for women in the navy. However, deep-sea diving was still not seen as a job for women, mostly due to the sheer weight of the suits, boots, and aeration systems deep-sea divers had to wear.

At the age of twenty-one, having been encouraged by Kati's achievement, Donna applied to the Navy 2nd Class Diving School, held at the Naval Amphibious Base in Little Creek,

Virginia. She was accepted just two days before the program started, in January 1975. The training was super-tough, but Donna became the first woman to graduate from the Navy Deep Sea Diving School, and one of the thirteen graduates of roughly a hundred candidates.

At the school, her trainer, Pierce Chris, showed no mercy just because she was a woman, stating, *"The men don't (tease) her because she's doing better than 85 per cent of them. You tell her you want a job done and she is able to do it, without your having to draw her a picture."*[26]

She then went on to work with the Navy Search and Salvage Team but could only work as an instructor for the Submarine Escape Training Tank at the Submarine Naval base in New London.

She also worked at the Hyperbaric Chamber, treating divers who'd suffered with embolisms, carbon monoxide poisoning, and gangrene. It's also noted that Donna was her brother Gary's instructor when he first enrolled in the diving school. Donna participated in a number of search and salvage operations, and even helped to sink a World War II ship at Chesapeake Bay, which would serve as an artificial reef.

She served in the navy for eight years, eventually retiring from her military service in 1980. Donna then used her GI Bill to earn a bachelor's degree in education and a master's degree in psychology. She then worked at the New London High School for fifteen years, in the Special Education Department.

She turned back to all of the pastimes she'd enjoyed during her childhood, including swimming, being in nature, art, sculpting, camping, and kayaking. However, she ultimately developed depression, which certainly was not uncommon for women who had experienced the traumas of war.

Sadly, at age fifty-eight, Donna took her own life on September 21st, 2010. A close friend of Donna's stated, *"She was passionate about life and loved life. It is a measure of how deadly a disease depression is that it could get such a person as her."*[27]

What Urged Donna to Choose the Path of Adventure?

It is very likely her father's history as a World War II bomber crewman in the US Navy that urged her to want to spend most of her life in the navy.

The family did not have much money when Donna was young, and so she likely felt that to secure her future she needed to aim for a career with a secure income as a way of avoiding poverty, but also with the possibility of fulfilling a need to achieve something extraordinary in life.

The world beneath the surface of the ocean has enthralled people since time began, with all there is to see at greater depths still unexplored. Donna was clearly empathic and deeply concerned for the wellbeing of others in disadvantaged situations. Perhaps the peace, and the pressures, she experienced when diving to great depths served to bring life into greater focus, helping her to override fear and worry, leaving her better able to assist others along their emotional journeys.

Perhaps, sometimes, when dealing with people with issues, the atmosphere around her beneath the sea felt somewhat destabilizing, enabling her to feel the 'depths' of emotion which others she cared about experienced as the result of trauma. It could be that the pressures below the surface matched the emotional trials she faced when trying to help others. Either way, she enjoyed the quiet as well as the challenges to her own physiological systems and mental capabilities.

She was not afraid of death, for she knew that passing under the water would be relatively painless. Therefore, to her, it would have made sense to go as far, or as deep, as she could, without worrying about dying. This would have made her mentally strong, as the fear of pain or death are obviously two factors that hold many people back from becoming thrill-seekers or adventurers into the great unknown.

As with all adventurers, Donna clearly had the desire to accomplish something that either had not been done before or challenge herself and achieve something she did not know she could.

What is notable about Donna is how creative she was. Creativity also requires individuals to go to the deepest parts of themselves in order to create. She was very specific about how her home was set up and how she depicted herself through creativity to those who entered her space. She loved music, painting, and sculpting, and she also followed a spiritual way of life that saw her adhering to certain lore from past traditions, such as hanging the bottles from her trees to 'ward off evil spirits.'

Perhaps, when at those great depths when diving, she fancied she could hear water spirits or receive messages from sailors and divers who had perished under the sea. She may even have secretly believed in mermaids and wanted to experience what it would be like to be one. With a creative mind such as hers, it is not a silly notion, by any means!

How Would Donna Have Prepared for Her Adventures?

Once Donna had decided to follow her chosen path as a navy diver, she knew it would take a lot more than a diver's certificate and the required number of hours clocked under the surface to succeed. She would have had to learn to handle the heavy equipment herself and know how it all functioned, which she achieved through her training.

She was highly motivated and did not give up after her first request to become a navy diver was denied. Instead, she chose to stick with her goal. But, while waiting for approval of her application to enter dive-school from the Pentagon, she did not rest on her laurels. Instead, she took the opportunity to learn something in another sphere of the navy, by joining the ship-fitting and hull technical team.

Most importantly, the part of Donna's training which would have presented the greatest challenge was learning how to adjust to the changing pressure when diving to great depths in the ocean. She stated numerous times how difficult it was to wear the necessary diving suit because it was so heavy and cumbersome. In addition, there was always room for worry that the air system would malfunction. So, perhaps Donna spent most of her time learning how to remain calm, so as not panic should something go wrong in deep waters.

She too likely experienced embolisms and carbon-monoxide poisoning through trial and error. In this way, she would have learned how to best deal with those she helped in the navy. Again, she would have needed to remain at optimum health, so as not to face issues with blood-pressure or her cardiovascular system. Her muscles would have had to be strong and toned as well, to avoid the cramp that can occur in colder waters.

Each dive she made would have been an adventure. While the process of sinking into the water and the protocol that followed would have been the same on every occasion, one can be sure the environment was seldom the same. Her mindset would have been different with every dive, depending on the purpose and location.

Donna would also have needed to be highly respectful of others and even somewhat submissive at times, as her peers would have been men of higher rank. Doubtless, some of them did not feel she had any place in the navy at all. However, through being as personable and effective as she was, she gradually gained respect and was even thought of fondly by many of those she worked with.

It is important to note that Donna never had any major relationships with men that we know of. She was never married, and no major relationships have been recorded. This was possibly because she already worked in a trusting environment with men, or because she enjoyed her work and was too busy giving it her all to build romantic relationships.

Her passing was sad. As a woman who had achieved so much and displayed such bravery, she took her own life after feeling unable to withstand the effects of depression. One might ask why she felt depressed in the first place. It could be that deep-sea diving was as much an escape from reality as a passion for her, and the depression was something she fought to keep at bay throughout her career.

In addition, if one looks at the physical side effects of deep-sea diving, it could well be that she developed a chemical imbalance, or perhaps she had experienced a lack of oxygen too often, which may have led to some unknown brain complication that affected her mood negatively.

What Legacy Has Donna Left Behind?

Besides being the first woman to graduate from the Navy Deep Sea Diving School, as well as one of the first women to partake in navy search and salvage operations, some of her additional great achievements include:

- Being a member of the crew to sink a World War II ship in Chesapeake Bay, to create an artificial barrier reef.

- In 2001, Donna was added to the Women Diver's Hall of Fame.

- In 2018, she was honored by the Naval Submarine Base New London, which named an important locker after her.

- Donna was on the team that helped to test and evaluate the MK12 SSDS in 1976, through wearing the dive system's helmet. Her feedback ultimately helped to better the equipment, with her input being vital to its development.

- During the 1980s, Donna played drums and also sang in a band called Loose Ends.

- Around that time, she enjoyed the arts very much and went on to manage the lighting for a theatre group which focused on mental health issues through lighthearted humor, The Second Step Players Theatre Group.

- Donna also played an important volunteer role with a group known as 'Art Reach' which served to educate the public about mental illness.

- Upon retirement and at the onset of depression, she also volunteered at the Mitchell Farm Equine in Salem, caring for roughly twenty-five elderly horses. The executive director, Dee Doolittle, said of her, "*It didn't take her long to fall in love with horses. They need so much care, and she had so much to give.*"[4]

- Donna was also firmly against the US invasion of Iraq in 2003, and she even had bumper stickers made expressing this view, which others adopted as well.

While Donna may not have a long list of awards, trophies, and medals, her role in the navy, and more specifically, as part of the deep-sea diving team, was instrumental in increasing opportunities for women. She was, indeed, a woman who sought depth in life and chose to venture down every path that might bring her closer to a deeper understanding of existence.

Setting Achievable Goals

With any major project one wants to tackle in life, goal setting will be of the utmost importance. When we are first sparked by an idea, meaning when we first feel that *special kind of exhilaration* that manifests in our stomach when we think of doing something specific, we usually see the end-goal first.

Let's use the example of a young girl with the dream of wanting to become the youngest Formula One racecar driver in the world. She is only fourteen years old and so is not yet legally allowed to drive a car. But perhaps, in this instance, exceptions would be made because if she were to wait until she was eighteen to receive her driving license, she would no longer be 'the youngest.'

Let's assume she is granted a temporary license at age fourteen, for the purpose of wanting to achieve a new world record. She would be granted the license because she already knows how to drive a car—she was taught by her race-car driver father when she was just twelve. She has the skill, for sure!

One morning, she wakes up and says to her father, "Dad, I want to be the youngest girl ever to compete in Formula One racing."

Her father, understanding the spark in his daughter, helps her along by recognizing her dream and agreeing to help her make it possible. But Formula One cars are very different from normal cars; the handling is different, the speeds increase more quickly due to the greater power of acceleration, and the rules of F1 racing are different, too. And so, she has aspects like these to consider. Sure, she can drive a car, but can she race an F1 vehicle?

Many adventurers or thrill-seekers find themselves wrapped up in the end-goal at first; the young girl sees herself on the podium with a trophy and the media snapping photos of her for the history books. This feeling is exhilarating and will be the main motivational driver behind her actions that follow. And so, the first step in setting goals will be to identify the level of 'passion' or drive behind the end-goal.

She then would go on to consider the resources she has.

1. She knows how to drive a car already.

2. She will have access to train in a F1 vehicle.

3. Her father's friend is willing to train her, as he was an F1 racer himself.

4. She will be allowed to take one year off school to train. Should she be successful, she can choose whether or not to complete her academic studies or pursue F1 racing further.

5. She will receive backing from a sponsor so her 'dream' does not create financial burdens for her family.

Once she has noted down her available resources, she will need to begin to set a timeline of small goals to reach before aiming for her larger one. These smaller goals will serve as steps to her larger goal.

Let's say the date is January 1st, and she has one year in which to train. That would make her fifteen by the time she attempts her mission (still making her the youngest female F1 racer). So, she will have eleven months to train, as the F1 race she wants to take part in is in December of the same year.

She will have eleven months to train, but how will she use this time wisely to ensure she is not only able to drive an F1 vehicle but will be able to drive one fast enough to win?

She would write her own timeline, with the end goal as the header, so to speak. From there, she will need to consider all aspects of her end goal in order to take the necessary steps toward it.

Perhaps one way she would do this is by prioritizing her strengths and weaknesses first.

Strengths:

- Can drive a car.

- Does not mind driving fast.

- Has great concentration.

Weaknesses:

- Is afraid to push beyond her fear limit, meaning she is comfortable at 60km p/h, but does she have the nerve to push the car to 100km p/h?

- Has never driven a F1 vehicle before and needs to learn the mechanics.

- Becomes light-headed when anxious.

It's the weaknesses she would need to address first, meaning she will set goals to overcome these personal obstacles before reaching the level of training that sees her readying to compete against others who are more experienced.

Firstly, she would need to overcome her concern regarding driving at speeds faster than those she's comfortable with. To do so, she would create a timeline stating the speeds she wants to reach per week over a period of two months. She would begin by setting small achievable goals. For instance, she might start by driving at 65km p/h in the first week, then moving up to 70km p/h in the second week, 75km in the third week, and so on, until driving at 100km p/h feels like second nature—until she's as comfortable with driving at 100km p/h as she is at 60km p/h.

Secondly, she would need to consider a way to overcome the onset of anxiety should something go wrong. Keep in mind that light-headedness could be fatal when travelling at 100km p/h. So, she would need to train her mind during the initial stages of her training as well, which would be referred to as psychological training. She would need to gradually make her way up to her desired speed, rewarding herself each time she succeeds in hitting her target. Of course, she would feel proud of herself for moving from 60 to 65, for example, but in order to ingrain this achievement into her psyche so as to overcome any angst in future, she would need a reinforcer. In this instance, a good reinforce might be that she gets to go abseiling if she reaches her goal.

Why abseiling, one might ask? The reinforcer would need to match the bravery she required to overcome the angst. It would need to be exhilarating yet safe, thus reinforcing her nerves. By choosing a fun activity that also requires bravery and nerve and accomplishing that task despite how nervous she was at the start, she would begin to feel she can do these 'daring things,' that she is capable of defeating her own anxiety not just behind the wheel, but in other areas of life as well. On reaching the bottom of a cliff face via abseiling, the experience would help build her nerve and inner strength, proving to her that she is capable of so much more than she thought.

And so, at the end of each week, once she has pushed herself 5km p/h faster than the week before, she should take the weekend to tackle another 'daring' activity that will help to desensitize her to fear. In turn, this will make the act of *driving fear away* second nature. In this way, she will overcome the anxiety that can develop at the thought of crashing or getting hurt.

Finally, once comfortable with travelling at speeds much faster than she was initially used to, she would train to drive an F1 vehicle. She would learn the handling and mechanics, but now without any fear at all for speed or getting hurt.

Note how the increase in speed was very gradual. This is setting small, achievable goals in action. We set small goals to begin with because we need to feel the sense of achievement and accomplishment before moving on to greater challenges. Had she been told she'd need to jump from 60km p/h to 90km p/h on her first try, this would be too much of a challenge. If she was to crash, she would lose any nerve she had at the start for her 'big dream.'

Each time she achieves a small goal, the achievement is reinforced through an adventure (like abseiling) reward that demands the same level of bravery she used to push the vehicle 5km faster. And so, she grows stronger and more confident over time, as opposed to going flat-out before she is ready, possibly crashing and destroying any spark of hope she initially had by setting her goals too high.

So, always set small, achievable goals at the start, then compliment them with a fun and equally challenging reward.

But why can't she rather have a new hoodie or pair of sneakers as reward? The answer is because these are physical items that won't match the bravery she needed to feel to push herself beyond her comfort zone. The reinforcer must serve to match the feeling she had on accomplishing her goal. In this way, she only builds confidence in the feeling and is soon able to push herself that little bit further.

All of this would be done with the use of a plan or timeline that she will adhere to, using dates as milestones for achievement. If she maps out her smaller goals to use as steps to her larger goal, using time effectively and without unnecessary pressure and constraint, she will reach her end goal successfully.

When setting small goals, you'll need to consider the timeframes in which these smaller goals must be accomplished. One could say, "She only needs three days to push the car 5km faster." True, she probably could do it in three days. But when we set time-frame planners, we must always add in an element to cover unpredictable events. For instance, it could be raining on two of those three days, which means she will not have given herself enough time to complete her first small task. That would interfere with the steps that need to follow, thus preventing her from reaching her desired end-goal on time.

So, it would be better to give herself five days in which to meet her first small goal instead of three, to be sure the small goal can be met on time. If she manages to complete her task in the first three days of the designated five, she could choose to have two rest days, or even repeat the step for the smaller goal once or twice more in those two free days. There is never anything wrong with 'over-training'!

This is just one example of how someone like this young girl would need to prepare for her dream end-goal.

Huge adventures like climbing Mount Everest, for example, cannot be attempted without the right training. Doing one mountain hike in warm weather does not amount to sufficient training needed to climb Everest. You would need to be able to handle below-freezing temperatures, work on your breathing, work on what to do when panic sets in learn how best to handle nervousness in companion climbers so as to not be affected by their anxiety should they become fearful. These are only a handful of the aspects one would need to consider when tackling such a dangerous adventure.

In conclusion, the importance of setting smaller, achievable goals at the start, as a way to reach your larger goal, is paramount. Never attempt large goals at the start, as by doing so you risk failure more readily, which could end up with you abandoning your dream altogether.

Always consider your strengths and weaknesses at first, then tackle your weaknesses before anything else, as your weaknesses are what you need to work on so they do not stand in your way in future.

Reward yourself with reinforcers that create similar feelings to those you experienced during your attempt to reach your small goal. By doing so, you associate fun with the level of adrenaline or fear you felt when tackling your first step, which should obviously require you to step out of your comfort zone.

This is how we progress in life, by always pushing ourselves just that little bit further until we finally feel confident enough to take on the end-goal challenge that will see us reach our dreams.

Conclusion

Never Lose Your Spirit for Adventure

Adventurers are a 'different kind' of human! When we are young, we have very few fears, but as we get older we face experiences that may serve to drive us towards being more cautious, perhaps even frightened of trying new things.

When we become frightened to try new things, we can learn to either overcome this fear, or we can be led by it. FEAR itself is a word that can be broken down into its individual letters as an aide memoire; **F**alse **E**vidence **A**ppearing **R**eal.

Sure, sometimes our senses do not lie, and we should listen to our senses and intuition chemistry. For example, if you see a shark in the water, it is probably not a good idea to go swimming. But to fear the chance of a shark being there, without having seen one with your own eyes, could be a waste of an opportunity at going swimming.

We are born adventurers, in the sense that when we are young the world is still new to us, and we want to experience everything we can. New experiences help us to grow, and this goes especially for *challenging* experiences. When we overcome challenges we feel victorious and triumphant over our own doubt in ourselves. When we jump from that high board and dive into a pool, after having spent at least half an hour trying to pluck up the courage, we shout as we emerge from the water, in excitement and joy for what we have achieved.

And this is the spirit that drives adventurous people. Not only is it in the discovery of something or someplace new, it is the discovery that we are capable of so much more than we first believed.

There are many among us who do not feel it is right to sit in one place, in an office or at a computer, for all of our lives. Granted, not everyone has the finances to achieve all of their dreams, but this does not mean they cannot pursue smaller dreams which are achievable with their available resources.

You do not have to be the first to do anything, and you do not have to accomplish new world records just to be adventurous. Being adventurous can be accomplished through something as simple as taking your dog into the forest in search of mushrooms, or even swimming in a lake with snorkel and goggles, in hope of finding hidden treasure.

It is this spirit of adventure that keeps most of us alive, the idea that there is always something new to discover, if not in the world then within ourselves. We were not born to do the same things day after day. We would never grow as people or in courage if we did this. And so, we keep our spirits alive with new ideas, adventures, and possibilities—that really are endless—as a way to enjoy life to the fullest. Then, when the time comes when we are no longer able to physically do the things we want to so easily, we can say we lived. And these days, luckily for us, we have videos and photographs to prove it!

Go on—rekindle your spirt of adventure within. Start small if you must, by remembering how it feels to be a child in search of exhilaration and vitality. From there, not even the sky is the limit—especially if you want to go to the moon or Mars!

Good luck and fly high!

Thank You

Thank you for reading this book!

If you would like to help authors like me, it would be very helpful if you would be kind enough to leave a review as it makes all the hard work worthwhile.

Many thanks, I very much appreciate it!

· ❤ · ❤ · ❤ · ❤ · ❤ ·

Read More

An uplifting guide of innovative female entrepreneurs encouraging girls and young women to follow their dreams.

About the Author

Ariana Smith is a financial expert, entrepreneur, and writer. Her many years of professional and personal experience through motherhood have nurtured in her a passion for telling inspiring stories to children, teens, and young adults.

She is passionate about empowering young readers to embrace their own identities. Ariana believes in instilling timeless values through history and literature; her mission is to help young generations find their purpose and develop self-confidence and skills that will help them lead fulfilling lives doing what they love.

Ariana's books are written in simple and engaging language and can be read independently by children, teens, or their parents. Her work has proved especially valuable to young readers seeking to develop critical thinking skills.

When she's not writing, you will find Ariana reading, cooking, or spending time with her beloved husband and their three beautiful children.

Visit Ariana's website to learn more. Sign-up to her newsletter to stay connected and get her upcoming books for free!

www.ariana-smith.com

1. Stoddart, Anna M, (1906) The Life of Isabella Bird, Mrs Bishop: London, J. Murray OCLC 4138739
2. wikipedia.org - Isabelle Bird - Travels in middle life
3. victorianweb.org – Isabella Bird (1832-1904): Traveller, Travel Writer and Photographer, Part I
4. bbc.com - Isabella Bird: Britain's forgotten female Victorian adventurer
5. racingnelliebly.com - Maria Spelterini Celebrated American Independence Week Walking Tightropes Across Niagara Falls While Wearing Peach Baskets - Maria Spelterini Defined The Year of The Woman
6. nflibrary.ca - Life of lady wire walker shrouded in mystery / Spelterini, Maria
7. Ibid
8. atlasobscura.com - Annie Londonderry Barely Knew How to Ride a Bike When She Set Off Around the World
9. Ibid
10. annielondonderry.com - Spin: A Novel By Peter Zheutlin
11. Ibid
12. airandspace.si.edu - Smithsonian institute - Georgia "Tiny" Broadwick's Parachute, Mar 12, 2015
13. Ibid
14. Ibid
15. earlyaviators.com, Georgia "Tiny" Broadwick, 1893-1978
16. dreambigseries.com - Eva Dickson
17. historiskt.wordpress.com - Eva Dickson's adventurous 1930s
18. wams.nyhistory.org - Life Story: Gertrude Ederle (1906–2003) - Olympian and International Swimming Phenomenon
19. history.com – History Stories - The First Woman to Swim the English Channel Beat the Men's Record by Two Hours
20. Ibid

21. medium.com - Krystyna Chojnowska-Liskiewicz - The Most Outstanding Polish Sailor Of All Time - Life attitude
22. npr.org - Japanese Climber Junko Tabei, First Woman To Conquer Mount Everest, Dies At 77
23. Ibid
24. wikipedia.org - "International Astronomical Union Names for Features on Pluto." International Astronomical Union Gazetteer of Planetary Nomenclature.
25. courant.com - Donna Tobias Bravely Swam Against The Tide
26. coffeeordie.com - Donna Tobias: The 1st Female Deep Sea Diver In US Military History
27. courant.com - Donna Tobias Bravely Swam Against The Tide
28. Ibid

References

airandspace.si.edu (Smithsonian institute), Georgia "Tiny" Broadwick's Parachute
airandspace.si.edu/stories/editorial/georgia-%"tiny"-broadwicks-parachute#

annielondonderry.com, Annie Londonderry - The First Woman to Bicycle Around the World

asmof.org, Women's History Month: the Incredible Story of Georgia "Tiny" Broadwick
asomf.org/womens-history-month-the-incredible-story-of-georgia-tiny-broadwick/

atlasobscura.com, Annie Londonderry Barely Knew How to Ride a Bike When She Set Off Around the World
atlasobscura.com/articles/annie-kopchovsky-londonderry-cyclist

bbc.com, Isabella Bird: Britain's forgotten female Victorian adventurer
bbc.com/news/uk-england-york-north-yorkshire-63735816

biography.com, Gertrude Ederle
biography.com/athletes/gertrude-ederle

REFERENCES 139

blog.nationalmuseum.com, The first female Olympic champion
blog.nationalmuseum.ch/en/2021/07/the-first-female-olympic-champion/

britannica.com, Gertrude Ederle American swimmer
britannica.com/biography/Gertrude-Ederle

circusesandsideshows.com, Maria Spelterini
circusesandsideshows.com/performers/mariaspelterini.html

coffeeordie.com, Coffee or Die Magazine - Donna Tobias: The 1st Female Deep Sea Diver in US Military History
coffeeordie.com/donna-tobias/

courant.com, Donna Tobias Bravely Swam Against The Tide
courant.com/2010/12/19/donna-tobias-bravely-swam-against-the-tide/

culture.pl, Meet Krystyna Chojnowska-Liskiewicz: The First Woman to Sail Around the World Solo
culture.pl/en/article/meet-krystyna-chojnowska-liskiewicz-the-first-woman-to-sail-around-the-world-solo

dreambigseries.com, Eva Dickson
dream-big-series.com/eva-dickson/index.html

earlyaviators.com, Georgia "Tiny" Broadwick, 1893-1978
earlyaviators.com/ebroadwi.htm

encyclopedia.com, Chojnowska-Liskiewicz, Krystyna
encyclopedia.com/women/encyclopedias-almanacs-transcripts-and-maps/chojnowska-liskiewicz-krystyna-1937

encyclopedia.com, Tabei, Junko
encyclopedia.com/women/encyclopedias-almanacs-transcripts-and-maps/tabei-junko-1939

foundationforwomanwarriors.org, Foundation For Women Warriors – Donna Tobias, U.S. Navy
foundationforwomenwarriors.org/donna-tobias-u-s-navy/

frankyinnewyork.com, Maria Spelterini
frankyinnewyork.com/stories/maria-spelterini/

historiskt.wordpress.com, Eva Dickson's adventurous 1930s
historiskt.wordpress.com/tag/eva-dickson/

history.com, The First Woman to Swim the English Channel Beat the Men's Record by Two Hours
www.history.com/news/gertrude-ederle-first-woman-swim-english-channel

jwa.org, Annie Londonderry
jwa.org/encyclopedia/article/kopchovsky-annie

latimes.com, Los Angeles Times - Navy's First Female Diver Took the Plunge
www.latimes.com/archives/la-xpm-2001-apr-11-cl-49701-story.html

medium.com, Krystyna Chojnowska-Liskiewicz — The Most Outstanding Polish Sailor Of All Time
medium.com/the-virago/krystyna-chojnowska-liskiewicz-the-most-outstanding-polish-sailor-of-all-time-538f69d872ad

motorsportmemorial.org, Eva Dickson - Baroness Eva Dickson von Blixen-Finecke's Biography, by Nanni Dietrich
motorsportmemorial.org/LWFWIW/focusLWFWIW.php?db2=LWF&db=ms&n=1388

ncpedia.org, Tiny Broadwick, The First Lady of Parachuting
ncpedia.org/biography/broadwick-tiny

nflibrary.ca, Life of lady wire walker shrouded in mystery / Spelterini, Maria
nflibrary.ca/nfplindex/show.asp?id=193572&b=1

REFERENCES

npr.org, Japanese Climber Junko Tabei, First Woman To Conquer Mount Everest, Dies At 77
npr.org/sections/thetwo-way/2016/10/22/498971169/japanese-climber-junko-tabei-first-woman-to-conquer-mount-everest-dies-at-77

olympedia.org, Hélène, Countess de Pourtalès, Biographical information olympedia.org/athletes/61789

racingnelliebly.com, Maria Spelterini Celebrated American Independence Week Walking Tightropes Across Niagara Falls While Wearing Peach Baskets
racingnelliebly.com/strange_times/maria-spelterini-tightropes-across-niagara-falls/

sailmagazine.com, Women's History Spotlight: Hélène de Pourtalès
sailmagazine.com/web-exclusives/womens-history-spotlight-h%C3%A9l%C3%A8ne-de-pourtal%C3%A8s

skbl.se, Eva Amalia Maria Dickson
skbl.se/en/article/EvaDickson

theglindafactor.com, Annie "Londonderry" Kopchovsky, Audacious Adventurer
theglindafactor.com/annie-londonderry-kopchovsky/

totalwomenscycling.com, Annie Londonderry: 10 Facts You Didn't Know
totalwomenscycling.com/lifestyle/10-facts-annie-londonderry

wams.nyhistory.org - Life Story: Gertrude Ederle (1906-2003)
wams.nyhistory.org/confidence-and-crises/jazz-age/gertrude-ederle/

victorianweb.org, Isabella Bird (1832-1904): Traveller, Travel Writer and Photographer, Part I
victorianweb.org/history/explorers/bird.html

wikipedia.org, Annie Cohen Kopchovsky - Wikipedia
en.wikipedia.org/wiki/Annie_Londonderry

wikipedia.org, Donna Tobias - Wikipedia
en.wikipedia.org/wiki/Donna_Tobias

wikipedia.org, Eva Dickson - Wikipedia
en.wikipedia.org/wiki/Eva_Dickson

wikipedia.org, Gertrude Ederle - Wikipedia
en.wikipedia.org/wiki/Gertrude_Ederle

wikipedia.org, Isabella Lucy Bird - Wikipedia
en.wikipedia.org/wiki/Isabella_Bird

wikipedia.org, Isabella Maria Spelterini - Wikipedia
en.wikipedia.org/wiki/Maria_Spelterini

wikipedia.org, Junko Tabei - Wikipedia
en.wikipedia.org/wiki/Junko_Tabei

wikipedia.org, Krystyna Chojnowska - Wikipedia
en.wikipedia.org/wiki/Krystyna_Chojnowska-Liskiewicz

wikipedia.org, Tiny Broadwick - Wikipedia
en.wikipedia.org/wiki/Tiny_Broadwick

womeninexploration.org, Annie Cohen Kopchovsky
womeninexploration.org/timeline/annie-cohen-kopchovsky/

womeninexploration.org, Krystyna Chojnowska-Liskiewicz
womeninexploration.org/timeline/krystyna-chojnowska-liskiewicz/

womeninexploration.org, Eva Dickson
womeninexploration.org/timeline/eva-dickson/

womeninexploration.org, Junko Tabei
womeninexploration.org/timeline/junko-tabei/

Printed in Great Britain
by Amazon